Reflections of a

Post-Auschwitz Christian

Reflections of a Post-Auschwitz Christian

HARRY JAMES CARGAS

Foreword by Vidal Sassoon

WAYNE STATE UNIVERSITY PRESS
DETROIT 1989

93 92 91 90 89   5 4 3 2 1

Library of Congress Cataloging-in-Publication Data
Cargas, Harry J.
    Reflections of a post-Auschwitz Christian / Harry James
Cargas; foreword by Vidal Sassoon.
      p. cm.
    Includes bibliographies.
    ISBN 0-8143-2095-3 (alk. paper)
    1. Holocaust (Christian theology) 2. Holocaust (1939–
1945) 3. World War, 1939–1945—Gypsies. I. Title.
BT93.C38 1989
270.8′2—dc19
                                              88-26798
                                                 CIP

This collection is dedicated to Lynn and Carl Lyss in gratitude for their friendship and their humane generosity.

Contents

Foreword

Harry James Cargas is one of the new breed of brave Christians who realize that the monstrosity of the Holocaust was a Christian tragedy. As a man, he is profoundly concerned with human dignity and human rights for all people. As a Christian, he shivers when rationalizing the historical actions of his religion toward others. He directs our minds to the establishment of Jew-killing as a political, sociological and economic prerogative. The fourth-century Edict of Constantine forbade the Jews to proselytize. In the same century, St. John Chrysostom preached that the Jews worshipped the devil, were the odious assassins of Christ, and that for killing Him, no expiation was possible; that it is incumbent on all Christians to hate the Jews. Shoah was no accident.

Over the centuries, through indigenous anti-semitic polemics, the church has grown—but has it? Let us examine the Crusades, the Inquisition, the pogroms, the deicide denunciation, the blood libel, the images created in the minds of Christians, debasing Jews, so that by the fifteenth and sixteenth centuries it was very easy for Erasmus to say, "If to hate the Jews is to be a good Christian, we are all good Christians." Shoah was only four centuries away.

Harry James Cargas tells us that Nazism did not start with Wilhelm Marr and Hitler, but came from a long, retrogressive ideology of hate where, in the final analysis, the Nazis felt righteous in the killing of the "vermin of Europe"—the Jews. The depth of stupidity, the combination of arrogance and ignorance, reaches the border of insanity. Even at the time of the Enlightenment, Voltaire, with his breath of extraordinary intuition, still had gut animosity toward the Jews and put mind to paper: "Jews, enemies of mankind, most obtuse, cruel and absurd . . . whose history is disgusting and abominable." The Enlightenment was a secular reality but could not combat religious hate. It is difficult to rationalize a Christianity so full of love and yet so full of hate.

Harry James Cargas factually tells us, as a Catholic and as a scholar who passionately cares, that the age of plausible deniability by Christianity is just another subterfuge. Essentially, what he is saying is that for Christianity to survive, it must eliminate hate from the Gospels and from its teachings; it must write a Constitution based on love, and a Bill of Rights for Christians and others, so the world does not shake in its boots every time "Onward, Christian Soldiers" is being sung.

Harry James Cargas is, indeed, a New Christian. He wants to tear apart the dogmas, cut through the myths, and rediscover the love that was in Jesus for all to enjoy. It is time for a second Reformation. If he, and others like him, can cut through the seventeen hundred years of endemic Christian persecution against the Jews, the term "collective guilt" will have no bearing on the New Christianity. As for now, Christianity and collective guilt go hand in hand.

Vidal Sassoon
Founder, Institute for the Study of
Anti-Semitism and Related Bigotries

Preface

There is so much to add to the text that follows. I have attempted, for nearly a quarter of a century now, to communicate the pain and bewilderment I feel as I am ever confronted with the reality of one of the overpowering tragedies of human history. Yet how are we to comprehend the enormous numbers of people who could kill enormous numbers of people? What of the millions who looked and pretended to see nothing? How is it that we do not live in a world saturated in remorse? Further, how are we to confront coreligionists who make excuses for the Event, or who deny the historical preparations, the theological rationalizations, the political actualities which seem to have guaranteed humanity's betrayal of humanity?

I have been uneasy in writing about the Shoah. But it is far more important to feel discomfort over the Holocaust than to feel comfortable in its shadow.

Each unit in this collection may be seen as a prayer. It will be immediately evident that I do not pray as well as I ought. Perhaps my skill will im-

prove. However inadequate, it is, nevertheless, necessary to pray.

Two brief notes regarding the text: I have made
minor alterations in some of the chapters in order to
avoid annoying repetitions (even though many
points, in my opinion, require repetition) and, recognizing that there is no such term as *pro-semitism*, I
follow others such as James Parkes and Emil Fac-
kenheim in not hyphenating the word *antisemitism*
—whether used by me or in quoted passages.

A Post-Auschwitz Catholic

This piece first appeared in the *Christian Century* and served as the Introduction to my book, *A Christian Response to the Holocaust* (1981) published by Stonehenge Books, a Denver firm which went out of business a month after the volume appeared. This beginning set a tone for the chapters that followed and is meant to do the same in this work.

To call myself a Roman Catholic is to describe my spiritual development incompletely. It is more honest for me to say at this time in my life that I am a post-Auschwitz Catholic, in the wider context of Western Christianity. The Holocaust event requires my response precisely as a Christian. The Holocaust is, in my judgment, the greatest tragedy for Christians since the crucifixion. In the first instance, Jesus died; in the latter, Christianity may be said to have died. In the case of Christ, the Christian believes in a resurrection. Will there be, can there be, a resurrection for Christianity? That is the question that obsesses me. Am I a part of a religious body which in fact is a fossil rather than a living entity? Can one be a Christian today, given the death camps which, in major part, were conceived, built and operated by people who called themselves Christians and some of whom—records prove, their own words prove—took pride in this work?

The failure of Christianity in the mid-twentieth century is monumental. Is it fatal? I need to know. This seems to me to be the main question facing people who today call themselves Christian.

It is too easy to say of those who lived and per- secuted *or remained "neutral"* in Germany, Poland, Russia, Austria, Czechoslovakia, Latvia, Hungary, Bulgaria, Greece, France and other nations during the Nazi era that, although they regarded them- selves as Christians, they really weren't. That's too smug an answer. One implication of such a response is that we who now look back and say that "they weren't really Christian" are eager to submit our- selves as authentic Christians. How can we be cer- tain that when the time comes for us to be heroic Christians (in theory, at least, the expression is re- dundant!) we will not collapse? All women and men are failures at their religion in some degree. But have we Christians, with our history of the persecution of Jews—with the Inquisition, the Crusades, pogroms, anti-Judaism and the Holocaust—established a tra- dition of failure from which there is no escape?

The reasons for my own personal conversion to Roman Catholicism from another form of Chris- tianity at age nineteen are not important. The act of commitment is decisive, however. I wished to share then, as I do now, in the many and great glories of the Church. I think it proper to say that I was ob- sessed with becoming as good a Christian as I could. Today it may be more accurate to say that I am obsessed with judging that original obsession. Was it valid or not? Am I a fool to be an active member of a church which proclaims love as its motivating ener- gy when historically . . . ?

I let the question hang. I'm not even sure how to ask it. Others will perhaps rephrase it as they too search. It is one comfort to me that I do know an increasing number of Christians who are engaged in such an investigation. To ask the question by oneself isolates one so greatly that it may be spiritually perilous. Raised in a tradition of fear of an all-powerful God who can punish the blasphemous—and questioning the validity of Christianity will be seen by some as precisely that—the question can be explored only at serious risk to one's spiritual health. However, some reflective Christians are at the point today in their spiritual development that it is blasphemous *not* to raise the question.

Silence, which can be holy, can also be sinful. Silence in the face of the Holocaust, I submit, is truly blasphemy. It is part of Christian teaching that God exists in every person. We dare not forget, then, that one million Jewish child-Gods were murdered by the Nazis and their collaborators in World War II. Five million other Jewish-Gods were slaughtered there also. An enormous number of non-Jewish-Gods were massacred as well.

My obsession with what I call the Christian Holocaust derives from the statistics cited above. Some Jews have been suspicious of my motives—I cannot blame them, given the history of Jewish-Christian encounters. Some Christians have been suspicious of my motives as well. Their suspicions are less understandable.

Through all of this, I have come to the conclusion that Albert Camus was profoundly correct when he said that "on this earth there are pestilences and there are victims, and it's up to us, so far as is possible, not to join forces with the pestilences." And Elie Wiesel was profoundly correct when he wrote that "he who is not among the victims is with the executioners." And Viktor Frankl is profoundly correct when he concludes that "we may learn that there are two races of men in this world, but only these two—the 'race' of the decent man and the 'race' of the indecent man."

Thus I must conclude that to identify myself as a Roman Catholic, in the shadow of recent history, is inaccurate, incomplete, even misleading. Culturally, of course, I am that, but spiritually I put on the mantle of a post-Auschwitz Catholic. It is in this concept that all of my work—indeed my life—is now rooted.

The Survivor

This is the text of a speech delivered in Madison, Wisconsin, where I was the first Rabbi Manfred Swarsensky Memorial Scholar at Temple Beth El, in 1982. Rabbi Swarsensky was a witness to the goodness of humanity and a well-known and influential figure in the wide community he served, which included Jews and non-Jews. A witness to the Nazi destruction of the great synagogues in Berlin, he established a new Jewish congregation, Beth El, serving there for thirty-six years. He also occupied the Chair of Jewish Life and Thought at Edgewood College, a Catholic liberal arts institution in Madison. Dr. Swarsensky earned his Ph.D. in philosophy and Semitic languages from the University of Wuersburg and was awarded honorary degrees from the University of Wisconsin, Hebrew Union College and Edgewood College. A selection of twenty of his addresses appears in *Intimates and Ultimates* published by Edgewood College (1981). This is dedicated to his memory.

The Six Million

We do a disservice to their memory when we mention them. The Jews murdered in the Holocaust must not be resurrected with inadequate words which will cheapen the experience of their sufferings and their deaths. But of course we would do a more sinful disservice to them if we forget them, if we fail to remember their collective fate; what was done to them, how and by whom. The historian

George Santayana has reminded us that if we neglect the past, we will repeat its errors. There is a Russian proverb which Aleksandr Solzhenitzyn quotes in *The Gulag Archipelago* which puts it more dramatically: "Forget the past and you'll lose both eyes." So we have an obligation to the Six Million. But it is also an obligation to ourselves and to generations yet unborn to retell the story of the Holocaust, to keep ourselves aware of all that we are capable of and to do so in a manner befitting the sacred memory of the dead—one million children under the age of twelve being among them.

However as we consider the dreadful events of the Second World War, we need to understand that the dead, some fifty million in all, were not the only victims of the Nazis and their collaborators. Many who outlived the war were also victims. Terrence Des Pres wrote a remarkable book about life in the death camps. He titled it *The Survivor*. Des Pres says of this volume, "My subject is survival, the capacity of men and women to live beneath the pressure of protracted crisis, to sustain terrible damage in mind and body and yet be there, sane, alive, still human." He argues that for too long we have honored only the dead with the appellation of hero.

It is to the survivor-heroes, the men and women who suffered the fate of the Six Million in all but death, that we give attention here. Their ongoing martyrdom exists in their bodies, in the pains they experience today from the effects of beatings, whippings, dog bites, rifle butts and so much else. This ongoing martyrdom exists in their spirits as well, as they undergo the agonies of nightmares, poor memory, nervousness, anxiety phenomena and the terrible, long list of psychic ailments medical investigation has discovered. Finally, this ongoing martyrdom of survivors of the Holocaust exists within the very souls of those about whom we are here concerned.

Just what have the survivors to say about who they are and what they had undergone? Perhaps we should begin first with a man who wrote one of the most eloquent books on the Holocaust, Jean Amery. Born of a Jewish father, Amery was raised in the faith of his Catholic mother. The Nazis forced an alien Jewishness upon Amery and he tells of the results of being tortured by them in his powerful work, *At the Mind's Limit*. With the very first blow one receives at the hands of one's captors, "he loses something we will perhaps temporarily call 'trust in the world.'" He adds that torture has an indelible character. "Whoever was tortured, stays tortured."

These are the people whom we consider now: the tortured, the survivors, the indelibly marked. Nikos Kazantzakis's words apply: "Everywhere you touch a Jew you find a wound."

It cannot be any real wonder, then, that in the death camps, tribunals of Jews actually held trials in which the defendant was God himself. In some cases, the Creator was found guilty of breaking the Covenant with his people by failing to protect them during the Holocaust. In other instances, the results were different. The jury in one trial concluded that what the Jewish people were currently enduring were the birth pangs of the coming of the Messiah. We know that many Jewish inmates ended their waking days in the camps chanting the prayer Ani Maamin—"I believe in the coming of the Messiah . . ."

But religious faith for a Jewish survivor is not easily categorized. Of one Polish Jew who lived through Auschwitz and lost his entire family, it is reported that "He retains a sufficient number of religious practices to remain the moderately observant Jew he was prior to camp internment. But his one expression of rejection or rebellion is, curiously, invested in making a point of smoking cigars on the Sabbath, 'regardless of the fact that I am not much of a smoker the remainder of the week. It is my way.'"

Here is the testimony of another: "I never think about God anymore," insists an attorney and university professor who experienced the ultimate agony of being forced by the Germans to choose between wife and mother, which should live, which should die.

> I don't let myself. I work, work, work, work, from the moment I get up in the morning till late in the evening, although I am above the age and beyond the need. I intentionally carry a full teaching load at the university and at the same time maintain an intensive legal practice. I never slow down lest I start thinking. I am an observant Jew. How can anyone be anything but, after what has happened? And yet in all honesty it is true I "davan" but I no longer pray. I can no longer speak to God as formerly; I speak at Him. Yet, I find that the synagogue and the mitzvot are as important in my life today as before—and as consoling. How could I go on without them? But as for God Himself—can you believe this?—I just continue to recite prayers. I never let myself think about Him.

Another survivor has said that he and others do not deny God but detest Him. Still another commented this way: "Our religion is proven true because it works. Our religion never permitted us to commit the crimes that their religion permitted them to commit against us." One man, without elaborating, gave this frightening judgment: ". . . the Holocaust itself was the Messiah. He has come and gone. And everything in the world is different."

One of the most anguished stories to come out of the Holocaust tells of faith in humanity, in life. There was a woman in one of the death camps whose job it was to bury those who died in the barracks or who dropped dead from starvation or some

other form of torture inside the compound. She piled
corpses in her wheelbarrow and carried them to a
disposal point. A young Jewish woman came into
the prison perhaps two months pregnant. If the
Nazis found out they would kill her immediately
since neither she nor her future child would be of
any work value to her captors. When the women
inmates learned of the condition of the new arrival,
they schemed to bring the child to birth as a symbolic gesture against all of the death which sur-
rounded them. They shared their very meager ra-
tions with the mother-to-be, they helped her carry
out the work assignments and they hid her in mid-
ranks during roll calls. They actually managed to
protect this woman until the day for the child-bear-
ing arrived. When the labor pains became intense,
the woman on the burial detail put the pregnant
woman on a wheelbarrow and then covered her with
corpses. The woman on death watch was the only
one of the prisoners who had access to the entire
camp, due to the grim nature of her duties. Thus she
was able to take her quarry to a remote corner of the
camp and help the mother to have her baby. Immediately upon its birth, the woman on burial detail
strangled the infant since the child would not have
been spared by the guards and by doing so, she saved
the new mother's life. After the war, the wheelbarrow woman said that she would dedicate her life to
having children.

Every survivor has a story. Otherwise they
wouldn't have survived. Some have many stories,
many close calls. Is it any wonder, then, that so great
a number are, in Dr. Leo Eitinger's words, "absolutely without anchorage in this world"? This Norwegian psychiatrist, himself a Holocaust survivor,
after analyzing the histories of thousands of patients,
concluded that 63 percent of all survivors suffer from

concentration camp syndrome, which means they regularly experience five or more of the following to a high degree: failing memory; difficulty in concentration; nervousness; restlessness; fatigue; sleep disturbances; headaches; emotional instability; moodiness; vertigo; loss of initiative; feelings of insufficiency.

Elsewhere Eitinger writes that

> One of the most unpleasant symptoms described by the patients was the painful associations which troubled so many. These associations are such that they cannot be discussed even with the closest friends or relatives. They can occur in any connection whatsoever, from seeing a person stretching his arms and associating this with fellow prisoners hung up by their arms under torture, to seeing an avenue of trees and visualizing long rows of gallows with swinging corpses. Children playing peacefully may suddenly, without apparent cause, call to mind other children, emaciated, tortured, murdered.

Add to this another incredible dimension to the existence of many survivors—a feeling of guilt for having survived. "Why me and not my sister?" one woman questioned. "She was a much better person than I." Others have repeatedly claimed that many great persons died while "we were saved" and they wonder why. What an absolute irony it is that these women and men agonize over why they were spared while Nazi soldiers celebrate reunions to recall the good old times.

There is not much guilt felt by survivors, appropriately, over criticism that Jews did not resist those who captured them. This is to charge the victims with the crimes. And the documented facts are, of course, that there was much physical resistance by Jews to the Nazis and Nazi collaborators. We also know that when Jews battled to break out of camps—utilizing practically homemade weapons against military might—and were lucky enough to escape, they were oftentimes killed by the very partisans they were attempting to join.

We are referring now to camp inmates who were hungry for hundreds of days, who were dispirited because they saw their families destroyed, who were covered with their own filth, who were freezing, who were numbers and not names. And some dare accuse them of nonresistance!

There *was* fighting resistance. But we must acknowledge another form of struggle which some consider to be on an even higher plane than that of physical courage. Here is Dr. Eitinger one more time:

> . . . there has been a Jewish religious tradition throughout the centuries, where "dying as a man" means something quite different from what Western people usually understand by this expression. To die as a man, or as Jew—for the religious Jews it is the same thing—means to die with the "Shema" and with the Holy Name of God on their lips, without resistance, without "falling into the abyss of the aggressor, namely, to kill just as he did." We may agree or disagree with this passive conception of life and its values "here and in the next world," but we cannot deny these people their last autonomy and the exercising of their last freedom to march into the gas chambers, singing "Ani Maamin," "I believe with perfect faith in the coming of the Messiah, and, though he tarry, I will wait daily for his coming." For them, religion still "was the essence of awareness of themselves as human beings." In order to avoid misunderstandings, it is perhaps necessary to stress that this applies to a minority of cases only, but for a complete understanding of all motivations the attitude of these few should be included.

Today, the survivor is as isolated in many ways, as before. "Without anchorage," is Dr. Eitinger's term. Holidays are often very lonely times. When

others are bubbling over about impending family reunions, the survivor frequently reflects on a family
that is no more. Once I interviewed a survivor who
learned, shortly after our session, that he was in-
curably ill. He called me and asked me to write his
autobiography for him. He wished to leave a record
of who he was for his family. The man was rather
desperate because his children seemed all of a sud-
den to be afraid of him. During the several months
we worked together this dying man came to the conclusion that the reason his three daughters shunned
him was because they were so afraid of the mystery
of death. Both he and his wife were survivors of Nazi
camps. They each lost entire families. Thus their
children had no experience of grandparents dying, of
aunts or uncles passing away. The children, too,
were isolated, indirect victims of Hitler's crimes.
The whole subject of the children of Holocaust survivors is now receiving great attention.

The sense of isolation comes on the *family* level
for survivors; it also appears from world events. Survivors repeatedly tell us that they feel a true sense of
frustration because they had felt so strongly while at
Auschwitz and Buchenwald and Treblinka and Bergen-Belsen (there are 146 such infamous names) that
when the war ended, the world would become a
much better place to live. Concentration camp inmates, we have learned, tended to idealize the world
beyond the barbed wire fences. "When the world
finds out what horror we've been through, they'll try
to make amends, people will be good and justice will
prevail," went the general thinking. The reality of
today's events proves that optimism to have been
falsely held, and isolation is reinforced. I have been
in Elie Wiesel's apartment on three occasions when
he has received phone calls informing him of the
suicides of survivors. (In some cases he did not even

know the dead—he has become a kind of receiver for all things Jewish. What an enormous burden on Wiesel's shoulders.)

Survivors find it very difficult to dialogue with the community at large, to dialogue on any meaningful level, I mean. Solzhenitsyn says in his first novel about the Siberian camps that a man who is warm cannot comprehend what it means to be cold. The same frustration is operating here: survivors feel they cannot make an impact on those who did not experience the unique, enormous tragedy which the Holocaust was. Add to this a newspaper story where a guilty Nazi sentenced to a few years in prison for helping massacre fourteen thousand Jews (fourteen thousand mothers, fathers, aunts, uncles, brothers, girls, infants, rabbis, laborers, teachers, violinists—fourteen thousand human beings, for which he's given a seven year sentence) has his term commuted after two months because he is ill and the facility cannot provide him with the proper diet. We can only imagine how that can add to a survivor's sense of global isolation—of betrayal by the world.

Yet most survivors go on. They fled Europe to new lands, without family, without friends, without funds, without even language. As one man recalled: "When I got to this country I was an instant dummy. Adolf Hitler took even my language from me." But they go on. The ideal world which they dreamt about in the camps never came to be. However, these heroic men and women helped create their own world, in a way, out of their Jewishness. They may not be certain what it means to be Jews. Yet they are certain that they *are* Jews.

The Holocaust—Fact or Fiction

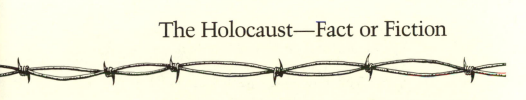

Those who dishonor humanity and betray the dead by claiming that the Holocaust never occurred have raised questions in the minds of some who are unaware of the history of World War II, indeed of the history of Christian-Jewish relations for over sixteen centuries. Those who do not know about the planned and executed massacre of Jews by the Nazis and their supporters may feel that "Where there is smoke there is fire." The smoke, of course, is a screen which so called revisionist historians blow to hide the flames of antisemitism. The article here initially appeared in *Way*, a Catholic magazine, published by the Franciscan Fathers, and later in the *Jerusalem Courier* (Springfield, Missouri).

Because I teach Holocaust literature, I am sometimes asked how I would respond to the lie that the Holocaust never happened. Those who don't know much about the subject can become honestly bewildered by books and articles which claim that the deaths of six million Jews by the action of Nazis and their collaborators are a hoax perpetrated on the world by Zionists who wanted to trump up world sympathy for the establishment of the state of Israel following World War II.

I know of dozens of such books, and a larger number of magazine and newspaper pieces in Europe and North America which have such a thesis. None, by the way, is produced by a reputable publisher, most giving their mailing addresses in the form of post office box numbers.

My first reaction, when questioned about these publications, is to ask if my questioner has read any of them. The answer has always been in the negative, usually stated thus: "No, but I've heard about them." The reason that I try to elicit such a reply is because I am convinced that any person who is not a marked antisemite will be able to see the fraud contained in such books and articles.

The most widely publicized such infamous book is probably *The Hoax of the Twentieth Century* by A. R. Butz, an associate professor of electrical engineering and computer sciences at Northwestern University. The work is a ludicrous effort by an author who contributes to Nazi-style periodicals, and is probably as obscene a work as has been published because of the author's conclusions and methods. He has decided that Jews were placed in concentration camps by Nazis as security risks. Under such conditions, epidemics broke out. In order to best halt the spread of disease, Jews who died under these conditions were cremated. Otherwise, not much else happened.

After the war, because Jewish men and women (and therefore husbands and wives) were separated into different camps, they eventually made relationships with others of the opposite sex and therefore did not want to reestablish their earlier family ties. So, in order to continue their new, though illegal and immoral, family arrangements, they went along with the hoax of the Holocaust. So says Butz.

Not a single Jewish European family wanted to be reunited after the war! No Nazi testimony at the Nuremberg trials, admitting to the murders of millions of Jews, is believable, says Butz. West Germany has gone along with the charade and paid tremendous war indemnities to Jews because by so doing, that nation will ingratiate itself with the U.S. government (controlled by Jews, of course) and thus gain enormous political benefits.

All of the literature published which claims that the Holocaust never happened is of this type. The totally disproven document infamously known to history as "The Protocols of the Learned Elders of Zion" lives again.

So I first urge people to read (by borrowing, not by purchasing) a book like Butz's. It is self-defeating through its infantile argumentation. Next I suggest these women and men read *Tyranny on Trial*, the best book on the Nuremberg trials, written by Whitney R. Harris, an executive trial counselor at the proceedings. Having access to documentation "unprecedented in history as to any major war," Harris notes that a major concern in the trials was to amass enough evidence to prove beyond any hint of a doubt that the Nazis and their aides perpetrated the almost unthinkable crimes for which some were being tried. Whitney Harris certainly gives the lie to anyone denying the reality of the Holocaust. So, of course, do many others, in countless books and articles. I recommend some of these, also, to those who are troubled by the doubters.

And then I invite them to listen to some of the tapes which I have recorded, interviews which I have been privileged to be granted with survivors of the Holocaust. I ask auditors to pay attention to the words, yes, but to give even more heed to the tone of voice on each of these tapes. Words similar to those I play can be read in certain written documents, but the pain in each voice—that cannot be duplicated. I have one tape on which a woman cries for nearly

thirty minutes as she tells me of sharing a concentration camp fate with her mother for four years,
and then seeing her mother perish ten days before
liberation.

A man has told me of witnessing the most horrid
camp conditions in a voice almost paralyzing in its
ghostly emotion; another's despair in telling me of
the death of his father at my narrator's feet, beaten
to death by an irate camp guard, is irreproducible. I
have many such unfakeable accounts. I do not, certainly, play them for show, but as near sacred acts of
proof to persons who are seriously searching for that.

Finally, I have a large number of atrocity photographs which I will, if the situation is appropriate,
share with others. Recently I spent time at the Yad
Vashem Holocaust Memorial in Jerusalem, doing research on the photos of that period, that event. They
are final evidence of the horrors of what many Jews
suffered—humiliation, torture and death. Anyone
who reads Adolf Hitler's plans for the Jews in his
best-selling and enormously influential book *Mein
Kampf* and who views some of these photographs,
will see the demonic relationship between the theory and practice.

The Holocaust raises many questions, some of
which we will perhaps never be able to answer. But
one question which can never arise is this: "Did the
Holocaust ever happen?"

It happened. There is proof. And I am ashamed, as
a human being, of that historical event.

Holocaust Photography

In *A Christian Response to the Holocaust* I wrote meditations on sixty atrocity photographs from the Holocaust. These were selected from over twenty-five thousand which I studied at the archives at Yad Vashem, the Holocaust memorial in Jerusalem. Each photo raised its own set of questions but I kept coming back to one: Who took this picture? Following this I could not help wondering if the photographer enjoyed the scene, used the camera as an excuse for not aiding victims or protesting in any way, and why this horrid memory was preserved in the wallet, the bureau drawer or the scrapbook where it was found after the war.

About forty thousand photographs of the World War II period, collected from all over Europe, are gathered at Yad Vashem, the Holocaust memorial center in Jerusalem. They can perhaps best be described as atrocity snapshots, with Jews as the main victims. By November, 1978, when I began my study of Holocaust photography, only about fifteen thousand of the total had been catalogued, so much of the material was of unknown quantity. In a two-week period, I went over between eight and ten thousand of the stills and it was a stunning experience.

War photography, as most of us remember seeing

it in *Life Magazine* for example, or in the books on the history of photography, was almost exclusively combat photography. Much of what we were given had a kind of artistic dimension to it also and the bulk of what we saw was taken by correspondents, professionals in the field of photography who made a living trying to capture what Henri Cartier-Bresson labelled the "decisive moment."

With Holocaust photography, however, a new dimension is added to the history of that form. We have thousands upon thousands of non-combat photos taken by nonprofessional picture takers. Recent books on photography neglect this part of that history. Beaumont Newhall in his revised edition of *The History of Photography* is unaware of Holocaust photography as are the editors of Time-Life in their *Photojournalism*. But a reckoning must be at hand. Perhaps the best people to come to grips with what can only be regarded as the phenomenon of atrocity photography by nonprofessional onlookers will be sociologists and philosophers rather than those who exclusively regard the art of photography. We are not very interested, at Yad Vashem, with camera angles, lighting techniques, etc. The questions that we ask are: What is happening in the scene? What took place just before and just after the shutter snap? What is happening beyond the edges of the photo? Perhaps most important of all, at least from a particular point of view, we may ask: Who dared to take these pictures?

We know that the victims in the death camps were not taking photos of other victims there. Who visually recorded bodies being shoved into ovens? What was the intended audience for pictures of murdered babies? I have seen a picture of German soldiers smiling underneath the bodies of Jews who had just been hanged—and it was on a postcard! Were such cards sent home by Nazi troops to their families as mementos of the glorious war?

Susan Sontag, in her jarring work *On Photography*, offers certain answers. She writes that "Like sexual voyeurism, it [photography] is a way of at least tacitly, often explicably, encouraging whatever is going on to keep happening. To take a picture is to have an interest in things as they are, in the status quo remaining unchanged . . . to be in complicity with whatever makes a subject interesting, worth photographing—including when that is the interest, another person's pain or misfortune."

Survivor of the Holocaust Luba Krugman Gurdus, in her book *The Death Train*, tells of the savagery of certain Polish people against the Jews during the Nazi occupation, "The Germans photographed the violence, using pictures in magazines and movies as evidence of Polish hatred towards Jews."

As if anticipating Sontag, Gurdus says simply, "The Polish police did not intervene." And here is Sontag once again: "The camera is a kind of passport that annihilates moral boundaries and social inhibitions, freeing the photographer from any responsibility toward the people photographed. The whole point of photographing people is that you are not intervening in their lives, only visiting them."

While Holocaust photography, with its mounds of bodies, its burning ghettos, its tortured and humiliated victims, its skulls and dismemberments and so much else, is a record of a terrifying historical event, it is also inadvertently a terrifying documentation of the recorders of that event. We will learn a great deal about ourselves as a (human) race when we learn more about those men and women who took the atrocity photographs.

1. Mass, naked humanity, being prepared for extended humiliation and incarceration.

2. *A suicide is recorded in the Warsaw Ghetto uprising.*

3. Children being taken to their deaths.

*4. The eyes of the imprisoned behind the chain link fence
tell the story.*

5. *This photograph taken in the Warsaw Ghetto is one of the most famous of the Holocaust photographs.*

6. The humiliation of women by the conquering troops was the topic of a number of photos.

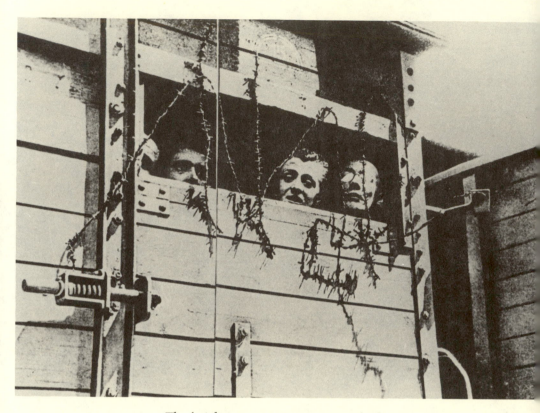

7. *The freight cars were never meant for human cargo.*

8. Prisoners hip deep in bodies.

... As They Stare into Mine

As told in this brief article which was written for the *St. Louis Jewish Light*, I was not the first to learn that Elie Wiesel was in this photograph, taken on April 11, 1944, the day that Wiesel and his companions were liberated from Auschwitz. Later, in a conversation with Dr. Leo Eitinger, a Norwegian doctor who helped to save Wiesel's life in the death camp, I learned the identity of the photographer, Sivert Stockland. Through the Department of the Army I have tried to locate Mr. Stockland but have been unable to do so.

It was not Elie Wiesel who told me that he is in this photograph. Dr. Livia Rothkirchen of the Holocaust research center at Yad Vashem in Jerusalem pointed this out. A blowup of this well-known liberation day scene from the Buchenwald concentration camp covers nearly an entire wall at the Yad Vashem museum.

Dr. Rothkirchen told me that Wiesel had been at the memorial site many times before finally indicating that he was one of the men in these bunks. He was only fifteen on April 11, 1945, when the camera of some liberating soldier snapped this picture. But he had already been deprived of his childhood, had endured the tragedy of his family, the tragedy of his

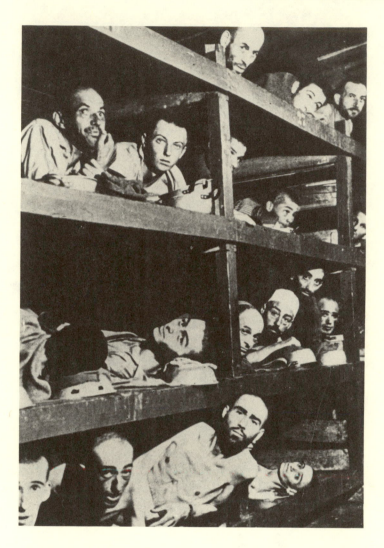

people, the tragedy of all of humanity. I, a close friend of Wiesel's, could not be sure which of the seventeen figures here was he. At least seven of the men in the photograph might have been Elie for me. It's as if they were reduced to a common image, one determined by hunger, pain, loss of humanity. The eyes of every man here tell part of the story. One is tempted to imagine that if we could somehow put all of the eyes together, in one mystical pair, we would there see the essence of the Holocaust.

Wiesel ends his memoir, *Night*, with the following four paragraphs:

> Three days after the liberation of Buchenwald I became very ill with food poisoning. I was transferred to the hospital and spent two weeks between life and death.
> One day I was able to get up, after gathering all my strength. I wanted to see myself in the mirror hanging on the opposite wall. I had not seen myself since the ghetto.
> From the depths of the mirror, a corpse gazed back at me,
> The look in his eyes, as they stared into mine, has never left me,

That corpse, those eyes, were preserved forever in the image of Elie Wiesel here, furthest on the right, second tier of bunks from the bottom.

Help Me Remember

THREE PERSONAL PRAYERS

After immersing myself in the study of Holocaust photographs one of my strongest needs was to pray. This
small selection of such responses was presented in *Face to
Face*.

Does this man need our prayers because he committed suicide? Or is it we who need his prayers? Lord of creation, You who made this wretched creature, we trust in Your mercy for this sufferer, and we beg Your mercy on ourselves.

Spare us and our children. From whom? From ourselves, perhaps. Enlighten us so that we may make a world devoid of persecutors, of victims, a world filled with men, women and children of goodwill.

Teach us to disagree without harming one another. Help each of us to see what it means to be made in Your image and likeness and therefore somehow to share in Your holiness.

The bones of mothers, fathers and babies, of rabbis, doctors and laborers have been bulldozed into
pyramids of infamy. How far from You have we
strayed, Lord, that this could have happened? How
long can we be allowed to go on living if we insist on
treating fellow human beings in this manner, sometimes even in Your name? How can we overcome
the sins by which human beings have damaged the
moral atmosphere of a world hungry for sanctity? Is
our earth a fit place for a Messiah? Is my own soul
such a place? Am I praying and working to purify the
world from hatred, from bigotry, from the kind of
ignorance which can produce a Holocaust? Dare I
pledge, in prayer, a lifelong vow to be alert to evil
and to fight in Your name?

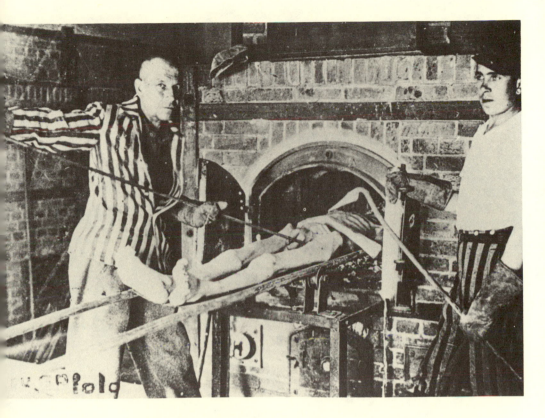

Master of the universe, can we be forgiven for
having invented ovens for human beings? Is any pen-
itential act of reparation possible to balance the
scales of justice and love over against the fact of
these instruments of annihilation conceived, con-
structed and operated by men? In the names of the
nameless victims of Auschwitz, Buchenwald and
Treblinka, I must ask myself what I am doing to see
to it that such monstrous events do not take place
ever again—whether in Cambodia, Yemen, Brazil,
on reservations or wherever. My God, help me to see
my responsibility and to act upon it.

Letter to a Friend

A teaching colleague of mine sent me a letter which began
with a sentence of congratulations for having added to my
list of Holocaust publications but turned into a rather long
challenge about restricting my research to the one tragedy
while ignoring others. Many of us engaged in Holocaust
studies have received such criticism on occasion. Often
the tone is friendly on the surface but has aggressive, even
antisemitic undertones. My response to my colleague's
letter, which was printed in *Shoa*, may be of some interest
to others in Holocaust research.

November 21, 1979

Dear Bill,

I want to respond to your letter in which you
express the wish that I and other "holocausters will
broaden your preoccupation" to other tragedies of a
genocidal magnitude, including the sufferings of
Irish, Armenian and other peoples. The implication
of your letter is that Holocaust scholars fail to express concern for any but Jewish victims of great
massacres. This is not true as I will indicate. Furthermore, your use of the term "holocausters"
seems to me to be a highly inappropriate slang term
lumping serious and hardworking researchers together in a very casual, sarcastic manner.

My initial reaction to your letter was something like this: If it is so important to you to delve into the Irish holocaust, or the Armenian holocaust, why don't *you* do it? Instead of using up both of our energies negatively in the kind of debate your communication has engendered, why not direct your efforts more positively in the direction you are suggesting that someone else take?

I do not know of any Holocaust scholar who restricts his/her compassion solely to Jewish victims of World War II to the exclusion of victims of other horrors. The whole point in working and speaking about the Holocaust is to prevent other catastrophes anywhere, at any time, to anyone. If you read much writing on the Holocaust, including my own, you cannot fail to see that.

It seems almost shameless to have to defend myself by pointing to my own publications on Vietnam, civil rights in this nation, Greece, Nicaragua, Korea and other areas, or my efforts on behalf of writers in prison throughout the world. Do you know of Elie Wiesel's efforts against genocide in Paraguay? But why go on? It is all there for anyone to see.

Yes, we have devoted more attention to the murder of Jews (the only case of victims on such a mass scale in history) than to others. But we have not ignored others. Yet we alone are being chided (incorrectly) for doing so. Has anyone scolded those who are researching the Nigerian civil war, Indonesian massacres, the Turkish slaughter of Armenians, the Irish "problem" to broaden their scope to include the sufferings of others? I have yet to see such criticism directed at anyone other than Holocaust scholars.

Furthermore, I have a very personal reason for concentrating so heavily on the attempted extermination of world Jewry. What took place there occurred in Christian Europe and in my view the validity of contemporary Christianity must be measured by our response to the Holocaust. Each time I attempt to pray, Christianity somehow is on trial in my soul. As you may know, I have written that I no longer identify myself as a Roman Catholic but as a Post-Auschwitz Catholic. That may give you some indication as to the background for my own involvement with Holocaust studies.

Finally, I must note the final sentence of your letter: "Perhaps you can judge which elimination was more excruciating." Why? What is the point of comparing tragedies? Each tragedy of the kind which you write is total. In every one of these, humanity is judged. The reason for such judgment is, I hope, obvious—to bring certain acts of humanity to the attention of the world in a way which will so move us that we will resolve never to behave in such a way again. Do we overdo it? No. As the great Catholic fiction writer Flannery O'Connor wrote, "To the hard of hearing, you have to shout."

I invite you, Bill, to shout with me, rather than against me; to raise your voice and your pen in opposition against injustices where you see them just as I try to do where I see them.

Peace in deed,
Harry James Cargas

The Protocols of the
Learned Owners of Baseball

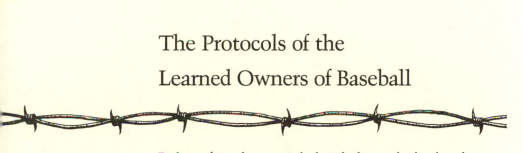

Perhaps the only way to deal with those who lie that the
Holocaust never happened is through satire. If I were to
appear on a program with one such person, as soon as he
uttered a word about World War II, I would ask "What
war?" and insist that there was none. If he can gra-
tuitously deny a historical event, so can I, using exactly
the same (lack of) principles. The title of this piece is
meant to echo that of the fraudulent document "The Protocols of the Learned Elders of Zion," which pretended to
prove a plot by Jews and Freemasons to disrupt Christian
society.

I can no longer remain silent about the great sports
hoax of the twentieth century. It is my duty to ex-
pose Babe Ruth as a fraud. He never hit sixty home
runs in one season. That claim came as a result of a
conspiracy among baseball owners to save the game
when suspicions about certain performers were high
among diamond fans.

To understand why the hoax was perpetrated and
subscribed to so unanimously, we must look at the
historical context of what happened. Baseball was in
great disrepute. The World Series of 1919 found certain members of the Chicago White Sox guilty of
betting against themselves and deliberately losing

the series to Cincinnati. Fans refused to attend major league contests and coined the term Black Sox to describe the cheating. After all, any time a player struck out or committed an error on the field, it might be because he had his money riding on the opposition. Nothing that happened in a game could be trusted. Maybe even the umpires were part of the scandal.

So the new Commissioner of Baseball, Kenesaw Mountain Landis, had the job of restoring confidence in the game. How he and the owners of baseball chose to do this was ingenious. I have discovered a secret document, circulated only among the administrative executives of baseball, detailing their sinister plan. It is titled "The Protocols of the Learned Owners of Baseball."

"The Protocols" is too lengthy to reproduce here, so let me summarize. Fans, we read, need to be brought back to the parks. To do so, their confidence in the integrity of the major leagues has to be restored. How? By giving them someone to believe in. Who would that be? A home run hitter!

Players might fake dropping the ball, fake overrunning a base, fake striking out, but they couldn't fake a four bagger. Why not, the Protocols advised, invent a hero, fabricate enormous statistics and hype the sympathy of the fans to a favorable intensity. "Our cause is just," one sentence reads, "our means need not be questioned." In other words, the Big Lie.

But who would be the hero? Babe Ruth was selected from a number of possibilities. He was raised in an orphanage and was eager to gain love and acceptance from the crowds, therefore he'd go along with the plot.

There were a couple of problems. Ruth was a pitcher, not a regular. And anyone looking at the bandy-legged overweight kid could see that he couldn't be much of a slugger. Nevertheless, there were even greater handicaps in choosing from among the other ball players, so the Babe was picked, converted fictionally into an outfielder and the rest, as they say, is (manipulated) history. Floods of press releases, filled with fantasy, went out all over America making stupendous claims about Ruth's Homeric feats. Sports reporters and editors collaborated on the hoax because good copy was obviously in their interest.

And before long, the paying customers began coming back to the old ballparks again.

Nobody of course, ever saw the Babe actually hit a homer, but everyone was sure that the Bambino *had*, on the road, in other stadiums, blasted the ball over the fences with great regularity. Eyewitness accounts of Ruth roundtrippers are to be given no more credence than "eyewitness" claims of alleged atrocities committed against six million Jews and countless others in the so-called Holocaust of World War II.

The baseball conspiracy might have gone unnoticed had I not stumbled on the secret copy of "The Protocols." It is my hope that with this exposé, I will earn the same praise due to other revisionist historians like Arthur Butz, who, in their books published from post office box numbers, show how the Holocaust never happened. To them goes the credit for inspiring this exposé of mine.

Faith, Hope, and Dogma

So often church dogma, which is meant to be liberating, is an excuse for limiting the Christian acts of Christians. St. Paul taught us to love, react from the heart; instead we are frequently urged to be cautious, obey the rules, to think why we should *not* do certain things. This is a perversion which, as the mystics have shown throughout history and in all traditions, puts lovers and hierarchies at odds. In my own small way, I experience this tension.

The headline was sensational, but accurate: "Where Was Christ at Auschwitz?" It introduced an interview I gave to a reporter which appeared in the *St. Louis Globe-Democrat*. The story dealt with my appointment, by President Carter, to the United States Holocaust Memorial Council. In response to one question I had said that "many Jews ask 'Where was God at Auschwitz?' I ask, 'Where was Christ?'" The letter responses which came to me were swift and generally very disappointing.

First to arrive was the Nazi hate mail. My experience over the years has been that there is a cadre of people just waiting for opportunities to anonymously attack, threaten and curse via the postal system. (Perhaps most memorable of all was the postcard I got about fifteen years ago responding to my efforts to abolish capital punishment in Missouri. The writer wished that all of my children got multiple sclerosis.)

Some of the vicious mail is crude, much of it badly spelled, all without signatures or return addresses. The epithet "Jew Lover" (which I proudly acknowledge) appears frequently. I am regularly assured that Jews will "disappear" from the United States soon and I will be dispatched with them. Often people try to give me information. This time I was told that Moses was "the illegitimate son of Pharaoh's daughter"; that the Holocaust was "all lies," that I would rot in hell forever and much else from correspondents claiming to be Christians.

One individual, typing under the name of "Truth," insisted that I must understand that "Catholics are 'not' Christians" (why "not" is in quotes is as incomprehensible as much of the spelling and technique in many of these letters), that "Catholics operate by Greek sorority laws that permit sex rites as per Caligula," that apostolic Greek women are lesbians (and the men, of course, are gay) and that since Hitler and his henchmen—Goering, Himmler, Moses and the Pope—were all raised Catholic. . . .

There's much more. What impresses one, among other qualities, is the huge amount of effort that goes into these communications. Many have paste-ups, drawings, are decorated, especially by a variety of colored magic markers. Some of the attempts at fancy printing and embroidered margins indicate that the senders must have many otherwise free moments at their disposal.

Later to arrive were the signed letters—a few of support, but critical of my theology. It was necessary for the purposes of the interview that I indicate my religious position. I have publicly, in speech and in print, said that "to call myself a Roman Catholic now would be inadequate. I identify myself as a Post-Auschwitz Catholic." A number of concerned and sincere correspondents reacted to that. A few insisted that my choice of designation was "meaningless," "puzzling," "contradictory," "ridiculous." In nearly every instance I was told that the answer to my question "Where was Christ at Auschwitz?" must be known to me—traditional theology held the answer. Christ was where he has always been, on the Cross, suffering with the pained, the tortured, the murdered.

And there's the problem, I believe: in the theology. I think that contemporary Christian theology has neglected to attempt to deal with the Holocaust in any meaningful way and consequently it has failed us all. Because of this, much modern Christian theology is near to trivial. I know of theologians who attended the Second Vatican Council who argued over whether or not Jesus' mother Mary had a menstrual cycle; a priest in my parish spoke from the pulpit on why it's a sin for men to wear bermuda shorts—and so much more of no real consequence to any congregation. (I have never heard a homily on the Holocaust or against anti-Judaism, although I've heard some pulpit words which were perilously close to condemning Jews for being solely responsible for Jesus' death.)

The fact is that about twelve million people were annihilated in the death camps. Half of them were Jews who were destroyed only because they were Jews. Jewish children, not yet conceived in 1943, were already condemned to death years before they were born. Approximately one million of the Jews murdered by the Nazis and their collaborators were under the age of twelve. And very probably every killer was baptized in the Christian faith. Every one. Why aren't our theologians dealing with that?

Is history the revelation of God's plan for humanity as has been traditionally taught by the Church? Then how does this massacre of Christ's own people, of God's chosen, fit into this schema? What kind of a God is it to whom we are asked to dedicate our allegiance?

Is there a conspiracy to hide a loving God from us in order to justify a theology which, to support its claim to being a science, somehow tries to mold everything into a pattern of consistency? Let me address this question through an example.

Recently I attended a luncheon at which Rabbi Marc Tannenbaum, National Director for Interreligious Affairs for the American Jewish Committee, spoke to forty religious leaders. During the question period, a Protestant pastor said that he was troubled by a problem which he wanted to share. Noting that through years of working with a rabbi, who was also at the meeting, "I have come to admire, respect and, yes, love this Jewish man. But I very much believe that Jesus is the Messiah." He wondered aloud what his attitude, as a Christian, ought to be towards the rabbi. This sincere Christian was perplexed because, I think, his allegiance to theology took precedence over a natural inclination to love.

In my work in Holocaust studies and in ecumenism, I see many others afflicted (that *is* the word I want) in the same way. The pastor quoted above, and those like him, seem to have read St. Paul in a curious way. It's as if he talked about "Faith, Hope and Dogma; and the greatest of these is Dogma." The mistaken emphasis on law over love in Christian teaching, whether it be official or unofficial, is in large part both cause and effect of the Holocaust. Unless we Christians face this critical issue, we may doom ourselves and our posterity. God have mercy on us.

To Excommunicate Adolf Hitler

As a Catholic in Nazi Germany, if you fought a duel, divorced and remarried, or propositioned a priest in the confessional, you would have been excommunicated from your Church. Adolf Hitler, however, was never so punished. He died on the tax rolls of the Catholic Church in his nation. Some insist that by his acts he was automatically excommunicated but that is ridiculous. Public condemnation was clearly necessary here so that no misunderstanding could take place. Hitler is dead, yes, and so is Galileo, on whose reputation the Church passed judgment several centuries after his death, as a symbol of its attitude toward science. It is time for a symbol regarding the Church's attitude toward the Holocaust, as I wrote in the National Catholic Reporter.

The Roman Catholic Church should excommunicate Adolf Hitler. Although excommunication was instituted to isolate a living scandalous sinner from the Christian community, I think it is important that the Church break precedent and publicly pronounce against the dead Nazi leader.

This was never done while Hitler lived, although the Church has not hesitated to use its spiritual weapon of excommunication against women and men who divorced and remarried, stole papal property, fought in duels, voted against the Communist party in Italy, sexually propositioned priests in the confessional, and so on. Yet, while he lived, Hitler was never even forcefully scolded by the Vatican for his evils.

Posthumous excommunication of Hitler would have two effects, I feel. First, it would be a sign to our Jewish brothers and sisters—a sign of acknowledgment of our past failures and of an attitude of repentance for Christian participation in the Holocaust (and in the Inquisition, ghettoization, charges of ritual murder, expulsion from certain countries, expropriation of property and so many other crimes Christians committed against the Jews).

Second, the excommunication of Hitler would be an unmistakable message to contemporary neo-Nazis, Ku Klux Klanners and others that those who preach racial hatred and their followers are behaving in a morally reprehensible manner.

Adolf Hitler was baptized a Catholic and he was never officially reprimanded by the Church for his acts. His blueprint for Nazi policies, *Mein Kampf*, was never listed in Rome's *Index of Prohibited Books*—although the far less dangerous works of Jean-Paul Sartre and Andre Gide did make the *Index* in this century.

Hitler's attacks on Jews in *Mein Kampf* were so vitriolic, so poisonous, that they cried out to be exposed. Young Nazis today read that volume as a kind of scripture, just as their predecessors did in Hitler's Germany. The book was widely popular and made its author wealthy. There is no excuse that the book was relatively unknown.

The Catholic Church's failure to act decisively against Hitler and his regime is notorious. Many Nazi leaders claimed to be doing God's work in killing Jews. Official expression of moral outrage was absent. Belated as it now is, many Church members

beg for some such sign. Hitler's minister of propaganda, Paul Joseph Goebbels, came from a strict
Catholic family; so did the head of the infamous SS,
Heinrich Himmler; Richard Heydrich, who led the
Reich Security Service, was a Catholic and the commandant of the Auschwitz death camp; Rudolf Hess
said he took his Catholicism "very seriously."

Rome excommunicated none of these men. Jews
know this. Neo-Nazis know this. A posthumous excommunication would be a message to both of these
groups. More important, perhaps, it would reaffirm
moral leadership by the Church to fill the void left
by its silence during World War II.

Canonize Dietrich Bonhoeffer

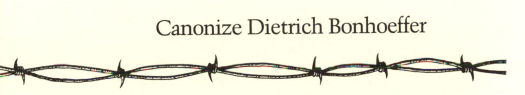

Ours is an era of ecumenical and interfaith movement.
Such healing could gain great momentum from a dramatic
gesture such as is here suggested. This article was initially
printed in the *National Catholic Reporter* and is dedicated
to Matthew Madden, our son-in-law who makes us proud.

In concluding his article on St. Maximilian Kolbe's
"doubtful spirituality," Peter Hebblethwaite la-
ments that another victim of the Nazis deserving
great honor, Pastor Dietrich Bonhoeffer, "will not be
canonized because he was a Lutheran."

I would like to suggest that the Vatican consider
actually canonizing this great Protestant martyr. In
what could become one of the most generous ecumenical acts in history, the Catholic Church would
thereby outspokenly recognize a Protestant who sacrificed his life in great measure for work he did on
behalf of Jews. This would be particularly fitting in
light of Kolbe's newly proclaimed sanctity, even
though the specter of anti-Judaism was raised—and
not satisfactorily dismissed—in certain publications
with which Kolbe was associated.

The Vatican record concerning Christian-Jewish
relations historically is not an enviable one; we have

only to think of the Crusades, the Inquisition and the paralysis during the Holocaust—and there has been so much more. Here would be a meaningful symbolic gesture indicating to the world generally, and to Jews in particular, that with the canonization of Bonhoeffer the current Vatican announces a true attitude toward Jewish brothers and sisters—and of course toward Protestant Christians as well.

There is precedent for such an unusual move. In 1964 Pope Paul VI declared twenty-two Ugandan youths who died for their faith to be saints. Approximately the same number of Protestant men were killed in the same massacre and their ultimate sacrifices were also noted. One of the main causes for the slaughter of these Africans who died in 1885 was their protest against the government execution of Anglican Bishop James Hannington in the same year. The situation bore the halo of ecumenism.

Surely there is some way for Rome to honor Bonhoeffer officially. It doesn't really have to be canonization; some Protestants might interpret that process as perhaps condescending on the part of Catholics.

A suggestion might be found in the Jewish practice of recognizing righteous gentiles, non-Jews who, at great personal risk, aided Jews during the Nazi era. These heroic women and men are memorialized at Yad Vashem, the Holocaust center just outside Jerusalem. Why not have a category in the Vatican for non-Catholics who were spiritual heroes?

This would concern some as a split with tradition, yet Pope John Paul II himself, in awarding the title of saint to Kolbe, broke ground. While ordinarily several miracles are required for canonization, this prerequisite has been waived for Kolbe by papal privilege. So the process is not hard and fast.

That Bonhoeffer is deserving of such honor seems

beyond question. He was among the very few to understand early the threat of Adolf Hitler. In 1933, a full six years before the Germans marched on Poland to begin World War II, Bonhoeffer publicly warned citizens of his country of what was happening in a radio broadcast which was cut off the air before completion.

A man of pacifist inclinations, Bonhoeffer agonized over theorizing about getting Hitler out of power as against actually eliminating this anti-Christ. He concluded that only a return to Christianity could save Germany, that religion clearly transcended nationalism and that the Christian "belongs not in the seclusion of a cloistered life but in the thick of foes. There is his commission, his work." So Bonhoeffer joined in the ill-fated plot to kill Hitler.

Bonhoeffer understood his Christianity to be rooted in Judaism. He had a great love for the Jewish Scripture and cautioned against an exclusive emphasis on the Christian Testament. He published a pamphlet emphatically opposing the Nazi practice of ignoring the Christianity of converted Jews. Some have suggested that Bonhoeffer's concern for Jews was limited only to those who had become baptized. Scholarship has proven that to be a false assumption. "The church has an unconditional obligation toward the victims of any social order," Bonhoeffer wrote, "even where those victims do not belong to the Christian community."

It is true that early in his career Bonhoeffer fell under a certain stereotyped impression of Jews. Protestant theologian Franklin Littell once stated that Bonhoeffer's deeds were better than his theology. But Bonhoeffer the theologian developed, as did Bonhoeffer the man, and recently Littell encouraged me to pursue this idea of suggesting Bonhoeffer's canonization. Finally, the noted Jewish author Pinchas Lapide has drawn this conclusion: "From a Jewish perspective, Bonhoeffer is a pioneer, and a forerunner of a slow step-by-step re-Hebraization of the churches in our days."

The prison writings of Bonhoeffer are among the most important Christian documents of this century. His book *Ethics,* much of which, incidentally—and perhaps for our purposes not so incidentally—was written in the guest room of the Benedictine abbey at Ettal, has been a text in Protestant and Catholic seminaries worldwide. His message of joy, of hope, of struggle, of responsibility, has inspired countless readers. So has the seal he put on his life—martyrdom.

Would the Catholic church consider special recognition of a Protestant whose life and death included a Christian commitment to Jews?

Why not?

The Continuum
of Gypsy Suffering

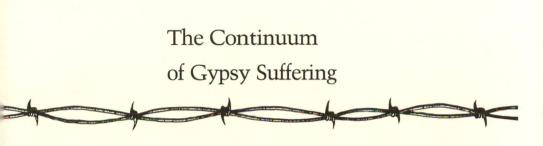

Gypsies, too, were subject to total annihilation by the Nazis. Much of their tragedy has yet to be heard. Here is one small attempt, from an address I gave at Kent State University in March 1988. I dedicate this to Susan Perabo, a woman of understanding and compassion.

Auschwitz. Torture. Deportation. Murder. Medical experimentation. Hitler. Dachau. Sterilization. Himmler. Racism. Mengele. These frightening words and names are all part of the Gypsy past, the Gypsy experience of World War II. Some of these words, like *deportation*, like *murder*, like *racism*, are, sadly, a part of the Gypsy present as well.

How did this happen? Who are these people, generally unknown, yet often despised though unknown? Seven centuries ago St. Thomas Aquinas wrote that we cannot love what we do not know. The same would have to apply to hatred as well. Yet many throughout the centuries have acted as if they knew Gypsies well enough to persecute them, to spread calumnies against them—who in fact worked hard to try to hate Gypsies.

This particular minority group is represented on every continent, particularly throughout Europe, although today, with perhaps a half million living in this country, the United States has the largest Gypsy population. Historically a nomadic people, Gypsies are portrayed as traveling in horse-drawn caravans and more recently in motorized groups. There is a consensus among scholars that Gypsies originated on the Indian subcontinent although the word *Gypsy* itself is a corruption of *Egyptian*, and they are called *gitanos* in Spain today. Swedes refer to them as "Tatars," the French have named them "Bohemians," in the Netherlands and in Germany they are labeled "heathens."

Their language is traced back to India, although the reasons for emigration from that land are only guessed. By the first millennium of the common era they were in Persia and they seem to have split off into two branches. One took a northern route into northwestern Europe, arriving there by the fifteenth century; the other group traveled in a southerly direction making it through Egypt and North Africa. By this century they had reached Australia, Mexico and other parts of the Americas.

Although there are several distinctions made between these people among themselves, they identify themselves by one generic name, Rom, which means Man. Therefore we have the terms such as Romani People or Romani Union. People who do not settle frequently become scapegoats for others. This has proven true for the Rom. On the one hand symbolized as the music-making, dancing, happy-go-lucky passer through, on the other the threat to property, health, and to children of any community since they are said to be subject to kidnapping by the nomads.

During the ninth and fourteenth centuries, many slaughters of the Rom took place in the Middle East. This tragedy was replicated during the Armenian genocide of this century. Throughout much of history their reputation was large and it was bad. It became a legal offense in many countries and at various times even to associate with Rom, and if such contact could be proved in a court case—whatever the alleged crime—such contact was often taken as proof of guilt. At the same time, however, at the social balls of the nobility, people came disguised as Gypsies and wives pretended to be fortune tellers.

It is written that the Christian Church at large generally rejected Romanis, even when they converted to Christianity. In Turkey, similarly, although certain Rom became classed as Muslims, they had to pay the same extra tax that Christians and other non-Muslims were burdened with. In Sweden in the sixteenth century an archbishop forbade his priests to christen Rom children or even to bury the corpses of the Rom of any age.

Trade guilds were closed to Romani and this seems to have forced them into living by their wits. Many resorted to thievery and other petty crimes, trickery and so on. It even became popular to associate the Rom with the blame for the crucifixion of Jesus. One Greek Easter carol will suffice here:[1]

> And by a Gypsy smith they passed,
> a smith who nails was making.
> "Thou dog, thou Gypsy dog"—said she,
> "What is it thou art making?"
> "They're going to crucify a man
> And I the nails are making.
> They only ordered three of me
> but five I mean to make them.
> The fifth the sharpest of the five,
> within his heart shall enter."

A Spanish Christmas carol has the Gypsies stealing baby Jesus' swaddling clothes, while some believed that the Gypsies refused to shelter Joseph and

Mary in their tents when the couple was fleeing to
Egypt. The Romani people originated, some chose to
think, as a result of Eve having committed an act of
necrophilia with Adam's corpse.

Other fantastic myths arose: Rom could control
fire; they had the power of the "evil eye"; they practiced cannibalism; all Rom women are prostitutes—
this last even though the tight social structure of
Romani groups allows for considerably less sexual
freedom than non-Romanies.

English law provided for death if one were found to
be a Rom (1554) and specifically anti-Romani laws
were passed in Lucerne (1471), Brandenburg (1482),
Spain (1484), Germany (1498), Holland (1524), Por-
tugal (1526), Denmark (1536), France (1539), Flanders
(1540), Scotland (1541), Bohemia (1549), Poland and
Lithuania (1557) and Sweden (1637). These people
were made noncitizens, therefore they were not under the protection of the law. Bounties, in fact, were
offered to assist in driving them out. As late as the
nineteenth century in Denmark, Rom were hunted
like foxes. In Moravia, some Romani women suffered
the amputation of a left ear; in Bohemia the right ear
was cut off. In a number of nations, Rom children
were forcibly taken from their parents to be raised by
Christian foster figures, as Christians. Nor is that
merely ancient history. Only a few years ago, in 1986,
the president of Switzerland, Alphons Egli, offered a
public apology for the fact that until 1973, in a nation
as apparently enlightened as Switzerland, Romani
children were taken from their families by official
governmental decree in a program which was called
"Operation Children of the Road."

In 1930, in Oslo, Norway, not pre-Nazi Germany,
a series of articles was published urging the sterilization of Rom. Not long before that, it was proposed in

Hungary that all Romani be branded. At no time were there large public outcries to resist such suggestions. When the Nazis assumed power in Germany in 1933, they did not have to enact anti-Rom laws—they were already in place. But the Nazis were not content with what was on the law books and in 1938 issued the Decree on the Fight against the Gypsy Menace. We must remember, however, that much of the foundation for anti-Rom programs had already been laid, including by the work of a Swedish sociologist, B. Lundman, whose racial theories were so excessive that he urged sterilization of all groups at the bottom of the social scale.

The slaughter of between four hundred thousand and half a million Rom (babies, children, women, men) during the Second World War was a result of centuries of persecution and an equal period of silence (at best) of Church officials who, at worst, actively joined in the calumniation of Rom throughout Europe.

While the Romani naturally supported themselves in ways which were consonant with their nomadic lifestyle, which was part-time, seasonal, off and on, they were frequently associated with fairs and circuses. And since they were regarded as outcasts, they often had to take the jobs which the native population turned its back on—then the Rom were regarded as undesirables even more. In India they became tinkers and entertainers; in Romania many were dogcatchers; some became executioners, hangmen in Bulgaria. They were slave traffickers in Brazil. In addition to this the men held jobs as smiths, musicians and horse dealers. The women earned money as entertainers, fortune tellers, tricksters and beggars. Even those who became more settled never became peasants or farmers but artisans, no matter how lengthy their stay in one place. Other kinds of occupations would have been inconsistent with their concept of freedom, a precious, natural concept for them—one about which most of us have little understanding.

Another basic factor we must recognize is that there has apparently never been one central authority accepted by all Rom. There is no Romani pope or king or president in the political sense that we know these terms. We must not be misled by the fact that international congresses have been held by Rom and that men have been figuratively crowned as kings. Relatively few Rom ever accepted the validity of such ceremonies. (There is an International Romani Union in twenty-seven nations now, represented in the UN.)

What political structure occurs is through the organization of bands comprised of from ten to several hundred households. Each is headed by a chieftain who is elected for life from one of the outstanding families. It is he who decides the patterns of migration, serves as the treasurer of the band, and is the spokesman for his people when there is a confrontation of any sort with municipal authorities. He is aided by a council of elders and the wisdom of a senior woman in the band. Her influence is strong because she represents the women and it is they who generally provide the greater portion of the earning power of the band. The Rom enforce a strong moral code based on the concept of fidelity, cohesiveness and reciprocity within the social unit.

What all of this indicates, of course, is that Rom, in their autonomy, have no message center, no central warning system, very little collective power. There is no such thing as Romani power. The basic Rom unit is isolated, poor, unsophisticated in the ways of national politics and military might, is incapable of generating a public relations effort to change the Rom image. Nor is it equipped to counteract rumors, myths, lies, fears which are spread, having no apparatus, having of necessity to turn inward in secrecy, hiding, with a distrust based on history.

Put in its basic form, the Rom fate in Europe has been two-fold, under the heading of persecution. First was enslavement, next came annihilation. Nowhere do they seem to have been more miserably treated, up to the 1930s, than in Romania. The Romanians compared their stereotypes to ours, Rom slaves to American black slaves. Said one alleged authority: "[Our Gypsies] are like your Negroes: foreign, lazy, shiftless, untrustworthy, and black."[2] Nowhere in current Romanian textbooks is the story of the shameful treatment of Rom told. These unfortunate people, Professor Ian Hancock, the noted Rom author tells us, were shipped to the Americas as well but he was unable to find a single treatment of this fact in over a hundred works that he consulted on the Atlantic slave trade.

The Rom were officially liberated in 1855, but here is an account of the condition in the next year after their freedom was supposedly granted, the eyewitness being England's Samuel Gardner, a Fellow of the Royal Geographical Society:[3]

> The children, to the age of 10 or 12, are in a complete state of nudity, but the men and women, the latter offering frequently the most symmetrical form and feminine beauty, have a rude clothing. Their implements and carriages, of a peculiar construction, display much ingenuity. They are in fact very able artisans and labourers, industrious and active, but are cruelly and barbarously treated. In the houses of their masters they are employed in the lowest offices, live in cellars, have the lash continually applied to them, and are still subjected to the iron collar and a kind of

spike iron mask or helmet which they are obliged to
wear for every petty offense. They are subjected to
other servile regulations. . . . they have the worst of
reputations, as robbers, thieves, murderers even; . . .
for myself, I have never regarded them otherwise than
a poor, outcast race, injured and ill-treated . . . the
force of prejudice is great, and the fears entertained of
these poor helots are the strongest condemnation of
their treatment.

As the nineteenth century was closing, a conference on "The Gypsy Filth" was held in Swabia. A
plan was introduced whereby all Rom in German-
controlled territories would be rounded up. Not long
after this, a Central Office for Fighting the Gypsy
Nuisance, under what was later to become Interpol,
was established—a bureau, by the way, which was
still legally constituted until its official closing in
1970. The fact is that when Adolf Hitler assumed
power, anti-Rom laws were still in effect from several hundred years previous. Dr. Hancock tells us that
"During the first few months of Nazi rule, an SS
study group proposed that all Gypsies then in Germany should be killed by drowning them in ships
taken out into mid-ocean and sunk."[4] The January
20, 1933, edition of a French language newspaper, *Le
Temps*, told of another proposal to remove Rom forcibly to an island colony in Polynesia.

In July, 1936, four hundred Rom from Bavaria
were transported to the concentration camp at
Dachau. While Dachau was not yet a death camp,
attempts to escape there were punishable by death.

In October of 1939, Reinhardt Heydrich, chief of
Security Police and Security Service, following Hen-
rich Himmler's orders, issued what is called the Settlement Edict, which forbade Rom from leaving
their campgrounds, or in the cases of those who
were more permanently placed, their houses. Under

Mussolini, who we know did not always follow the Nazi lead in atrocities, Rom were rounded up on a large scale even before the war began. Many of the men were forced into military service. They were assigned to Italian-occupied Albania, from whence they were permanently exiled, forbidden to return. Their families were allowed to join them there.

Inhuman acts took place elsewhere, as well. Donald Kenrick and Grattan Puxon tell us, for example, that "Few Gypsies survived the *terror* in northern Yugoslavia. The Catholic-supported Croat separatist movement which took power four days after German units crossed the frontier, inaugurated a blood bath. The victims died in what was popularly termed a 'holy war' against non-Catholic minorities. . . ."

An example of the Church's silence on this topic is given by Raul Hilberg in quoting Ernst von Weizsacker, who held several diplomatic posts under Hitler including the Third Reich's office of Ambassador to the Vatican. Of a papal representative who was weakly protesting the murders of Gypsies and others in Croatia, von Weizsacker wrote:

> The nuncio today groped around to the well-known subject of hostages, in order to determine whether a discussion between him and me about the question of shooting hostages—of late in Serbia—would be fruitful [*erspriesslich*]. I replied to the nuncio that, among all foreign governments which have concerned themselves with this question, the Vatican had conducted itself most cleverly [*am Klugsten*], in that it took the hint I had furtively extended to Papal Counselor Colli upon a social occasion. If the Vatican should nevertheless feel constrained to return to this subject, I would be obliged to give to the nuncio the same answers that Mexico, Haiti, and other governments had received already. The nuncio saw this point completely and pointed out that he had not really touched this topic and that he had no desire to touch it.[5]

In Poland, massacres of Rom took place on a large scale. Many of the crimes were committed by citizens of that country, some murders taking place when dogs were loosed upon the victims. However, with the exception of Austria and Germany itself, it was only in Poland that Nazi authorities attempted to seriously negotiate with representatives of the Rom. Nevertheless, little advantage thus came to the Rom since it is estimated that about two-thirds of all Polish Rom, approximately thirty-five thousand, lost their lives during the occupation of that nation by the Nazis.

Josef Mengele, the infamous Nazi medical doctor, practiced many of his notorious scientific experiments on Rom—he and the associates under his direction. He had experimental barracks built in the camp at Birkenau where research—torture, really—was performed on twins, dwarfs, giants and others considered abnormal or deformed. Robert Jay Lifton, in his book *The Nazi Doctors*, describes an important moment in some detail:

> SS doctors were . . . involved— . . . especially Mengele—in the killing of the four thousand inhabitants of the Gypsy camp on 1 August 1944. Mengele was chief doctor of that camp, and so active was he in the annihilation process that many prisoners I spoke to assumed that he himself was responsible for it and had given the specific order. There is evidence that he actually opposed the annihilation; but once it was ordered, he applied extraordinary energy toward carrying it out.
>
> Prisoner doctors who had worked there at the time told me that Mengele seemed to be all over the camp at once that day, actively supervising arrangements for getting the Gypsies to the gas chamber. He had been close to some of the Gypsy children—bringing them food and candy, sometimes little toys, and taking them for brief outings. Whenever he appeared, they would greet him warmly with the cry, "Onkel [Uncle]

Mengele!" But that day the children were frightened. Dr. Alexander O. described the scene and one child's plea to Mengele:

Mengele arrived at around eight o'clock or seven-thirty. It was daylight. He came, and then the children . . . A Gypsy girl of eleven, twelve . . . the oldest [child] of a whole family—maybe thirteen, with malnutrition sometimes they grow less. "Onkel Mengele [she calls], my little brother cries himself to death. We do not know where our mother is. He cries himself to death, Onkel Mengele!" Where did she go to complain? To Mengele—to the one she loves and knows she is loved by, because he loved them. His answer: . . . He said it in a common, vulgar way . . . but . . . with a sort of tenderness: . . . "Why don't you shut your little trap!"

Others told how Mengele combed the blocks, tracking down Gypsy children who had hidden, and how he himself transported a group of those children in a car to the gas chamber—drawing upon their trust for him and speaking tenderly and reassuringly to them until the end.

With adults it was a little different. Dr. Alexander O. remembered their protesting that they had "fought for Germany." Another prisoner physician, recalling a *Blocksperre*, said, "Whenever I see a picture of Dracula, I think of Mengele running through the *Zigeuner* [Gypsy] camp—just like Dracula. . . . We could hear the terrible crying from the beating and torturing as they put the Gypsies on those cars. . . . [On nearby blocks] they were crying and shouting, "We are worried that Mengele and his assistant will come and burn us."[6]

Another eyewitness account is that of Pery Broad, a functionary of the camp Gestapo of Auschwitz who had volunteered for the SS.

A motley crowd of French, Hungarian, Czech, Polish and German Gypsies came to the camp in the course of the next few weeks. They came with their children and their personal possessions. They were brought to a separate sector of *Birkenau*, called the Gypsy camp. Then, in March, express letters arrived

with red margins, containing further orders. According
to these, by order of the *Reichsfuhrer* all Gypsies,
"regardless of whether or not they were of mixed
blood" should be sent to work in the concentration
camp. The exceptions were to be Gypsies and half-
breeds who had stable abodes, were socially well ad-
justed and were holding steady jobs. This clause was a
mere formality and was never observed. It was precisely the settled Gypsies who were the easiest prey,
and so they formed the largest percentage of the camp
inmates. Girls who had worked in army offices as
typists, workmen in the OT [Organisation Todt], stu-
dents of music schools, and others with a solid background of steady and efficient work, suddenly found
themselves in a concentration camp as prisoners with
shaved heads and in blue-white prison clothes, their
prisoner's number tattooed on their arms. That was
not all, the madness went further. Hundreds of soldiers, who had not the slightest idea that they were
half-breeds, were transferred from the front lines, deprived of their uniforms and sent to the concentration
camps, just because they happened to have twelve or
even less percent of Gypsy blood. Those decorated
with the Iron Cross and other medals for bravery were
overnight sent behind the barbed wire fences of
Auschwitz as "anti-socials." According to secret orders, this should not have happened. Half-breeds, who
had distinguished themselves as soldiers during the
war, should have been exempted from the general
rule, on the condition that they consented to be ster-
ilized. But the majority of them were never asked to
consent, they were simply arrested. All were promised
they would be brought to a Gypsy settlement. The
documents dealing with the Gypsy problem were sent
by the Criminal Police Office of the Reich and by the
Reich Central Office for Combating Gypsies, and were
signed by Criminal Councillor Otto, Dr. Ritter and
Bohlhoff. About 16,000 Gypsies were transported to
Auschwitz.[7]

The final eyewitness to be quoted here is perhaps
the greatest mass murdered in all of history, Rudolf
Franz Ferdinand Hess, the Commandant of Ausch-

witz whose written confession is one of the worst
horror stories ever told. In this section he begins by
telling us of showing his superior, Heinrich Himmler, around the camp:

> . . . the *Reichsfuhrer SS* [Himmler] visited the
> camp. I took him all over the Gypsy camp. He made a
> most thorough inspection of everything, noting the
> overcrowded barrack-huts, the unhygienic conditions,
> the cramped hospital building. He saw those who
> were sick with infectious diseases, and the children
> suffering from *Noma*—which always made me shud-
> der, since it reminded me of leprosy and of the lepers I
> had seen in Palestine—their little bodies wasted away,
> with gaping holes in their cheeks big enough for a
> man to see through, a slow putrefaction of the living
> body.
> He noted the mortality rate, which was relatively
> low in comparison with that of the camp as a whole.
> The child mortality rate, however, was extraordinarily
> high. I do not believe that many new-born babies
> survived more than a few weeks.
> He saw it all, in detail, and as it really was—and he
> ordered me to destroy them. Those capable of work
> were first to be separated from the others. . . .[8]

The Rom story, a grim history of persecution, racism, annihilation and forgetting, has hardly been
told, has hardly been explored, has certainly not been
heard. Nor did it end abruptly with the ending of
hostilities in 1945. As Yehuda Bauer has written,
"The Gypsies who have survived the war continued
to be hunted and discriminated against in postwar
Germany. . . ."[9] Rom received nothing in the way of
war reparations. There is the known case of a woman
having received, for the death of her child at Auschwitz, ten dollars. Dr. Hancock tells of West German
officials rejecting the attempts of several thousand
Rom survivors to establish citizenship in the Federal
Republic, even though their families had lived in
Germany for many generations. No Rom was asked

to testify at the Nuremberg War Crimes Trial, nor at any other major legal proceeding involving Nazi atrocities against humanity.

Some changes are beginning to take place. In 1987, in Germany, Dr. Gabrielle Tyrnauer has said, a defendant in a war crime trial was charged with the fatal beating of a Rom woman.[10] In 1986, the German Bundestag officially passed a joint resolution on Rom which recognizes their suffering.

In spite of these changes, however, there are growing tensions as well. It is with a brief attention to this developing problem that I will close. The tensions that are becoming more and more visible are between *some* Rom and *some* Jews. I have deliberately made no reference to the Jewish Holocaust in this paper. I do not wish to make any comparison between the attempted genocides of both groups. It seems to be here, in such comparisons, that difficulties are emphasized. I would hope that any anger which appears be directed at the common enemy, at the Nazis and their collaborators. For Jews and Rom to have strained relations would be no less than tragic.

What follows is not nearly the complete story. But it has to be aired. Some Rom are upset, perhaps jealous, because the victimization of the Jews has received far more attention than their own tragedy. Some Jews are disturbed, because, they feel, the uniqueness of their Holocaust disaster will be somehow diminished if the nature of the Rom experience receives fuller attention than it is now getting. Both views are shortsighted. All tragedies have their unique dimensions. To acknowledge one is not to trivialize another. Certain Jews have to recognize this. That the Jewish pain has gained greater worldwide attention than theirs should not in itself make the Rom uncomfortable. Rom should be grateful that the People of the Book are thus paving the way for the People of the Moment to have their story—the Rom story—memorialized. For each group to ignore the other's tragedy, or to minimize it or be jealous of its notoriety would itself be tragic. The principle we must work from is this: What can be done to one of us can be done to all of us.

The man whom we honor specifically at this conference, Vidal Sassoon, has recognized this. What he has founded and supported in Israel is the Institute for the Study of Anti-Semitism and Related Bigotries. Rom, Jews, Armenians, Jehovah's Witnesses, homosexuals, Cambodians, Brazilian Indians, Kurds, all those who had suffered genocidal attempts, have got to work together in the interest of their common humanity. There is a need to note *when* the laws against one group were passed. It is less important to insist that laws against *us* were promulgated before laws against *them*. There seems to be no value in trying to prove that we suffered more than they.

Make no mistake: I am not advocating a universalist approach to the Holocaust. I minimize none of the uniqueness of the Shoah. What I am advocating is peace between the victims. There is sniping going on. In the name of God, in the service of humanity, we must stop it.

Notes

1. Donald Kenrick and Grattan Puxon, *The Destiny of Europe's Gypsies* (New York: Basic Books, 1972), p. 27.

2. Ian Hancock, *The Pariah Syndrome* (Ann Arbor: Karoma, 1987), p. 1.

3. Ibid., p. 39.

4. Ibid., p. 62.

5. Raul Hilberg, *The Destruction of the European Jews* (New York: Watts, 1973), pp. 440–41.

6. Robert Jay Lifton, *The Nazi Doctors* (New York: Basic Books, 1986), pp. 185–86.

7. Jadwiga Bezwinska and Danuta Czech, eds., *KL Auschwitz Seen by the SS* (Auschwitz: Pantswowe Museum, 1978), pp. 186–89.

8. *Ibid.*, pp. 65–68.

9. Yehuda Bauer, *A History of the Holocaust* (New York: Franklin Watts, 1982), p. 337.

10. Gabrielle Tyrnauer, unpublished address titled "Holocaust History and the Gypsies," presented at McMaster University to the Canadian Sociology and Anthropology Association, 1987.

Hochhuth's *The Deputy*

ONE GENERATION AFTER

In 1963, as editor-in-chief of the *Queen's Work* magazine
and pamphlet division, a Catholic publishing house, I initiated publication of a booklet to defend Pope Pius XII
from Rolf Hochhuth's allegations in his already notorious
drama. That booklet never appeared. As I studied the situation, I became increasingly certain that Hochhuth's
criticism was perhaps more valid than even he himself
knew. A generation later, I gave this assessment at the
Sixteenth Annual Conference on the Church Struggle and
the Holocaust. This talk, later published in *Shofar,* is dedicated to the memory of my niece, Alicia Remus.

It is very likely that no play in the history of world
theater has ever caused as great an uproar as Rolf
Hochhuth's *The Deputy.*[1] People have reacted to it
as drama, as history, as anti-Catholic, as not drama
at all—in varying ways—but people have reacted to
it. Now, a generation after the play was initially
produced, is a proper time to re-evaluate it. We are
no longer in an emotionally charged atmosphere
which put audience members in paroxysms of response *before* the curtain even rose; we are at a time,
in fact, when the play is not to be seen perhaps anywhere in the world. It may be that *only* now are we

able to approach *The Deputy* with a kind of distance necessary to judge its place in the world of letters.

The playwright has called this work a Christian tragedy[2] and certain critics have agreed with him.[3] To the charges that the drama is anti-Catholic because of the unfavorable portrayal of Pope Pius XII and other hierarchical figures that appear, the eminent Roman Catholic historian Friedrich Heer has written that this is clearly not the case, reminding, among other observations, that *The Deputy* is dedicated to the memory of two Catholic priests: Maximilian Kolbe and Bernhard Lichtenberg.[4]

The Deputy must be judged from two points of view: that of literature and that of history. Let us look at it first as a theatrical event. Briefly it is the story of a young Jesuit priest, Ricardo Fontana, who is horrified by Nazi atrocities committed against Jewish people. Because he has access to Pope Pius XII, Ricardo attempts to persuade him to intercede on behalf of the persecuted. The Pope chooses not to and Ricardo joins the victims and dies at the hands of an SS machine-gunner.

In its original form, the drama would take some seven hours to stage[5] and the author might be criticized for this impracticality.[6] Nevertheless *The Deputy* exists assuredly as much to be read as to be seen. (The fact is that many plays are more often read than seen. We have only to think of Greek tragedy, and French drama of Corneille and Racine, the plays of Shakespeare and other Renaissance artists, Goethe's *Faust*, and ask ourselves how many of those works have we read compared to how many we have actually witnessed.)

As an actual theater experience, *The Deputy* has been received unevenly. John Simon refers to "The preposterous Broadway version,"[7] Alfred Kazin has labelled it "a tract in dramatic form,"[8] and Walter

Kerr reproved the author for staging a play that needs an appendix—which the book has and the production cannot have.[9] Even the printed version is faulted by Robert Brustein for reading "like a German doctoral dissertation in verse. . . ."[10] Here is a sampling of what other critics have had to say: "Whatever *The Deputy* is as a moral event, it is not playwriting of the highest order."[11] The work has been damned as melodramatic;[12] Hochhuth has been accused of writing a bad play because his characters are weak,[13] his sense of the dramatic has been questioned;[14] and Hochhuth's oversimplification of complex issues has been criticized.[15]

On the plus side, however, is Susan Sontag's perception that "We live in a time in which tragedy is not an art form but a form of history."[16] She finds the Eichmann trial to be one of the most interesting works of recent art.[17] Hochhuth is said to have written in the tradition of the political theater and the first director of the play in Germany compared Hochhuth's efforts as successor to the historical plays of Shakespeare, Schiller and the epic theater of Brecht.[18] Despite its artistic and interpretive shortcomings, Brustein indicates that the published form of the play is a document of power and persuasiveness.[19]

Other commentators have noted that while the drama is flawed, it still contains considerable value.[20] Simon has drawn attention to the contrapuntal design of the author.[21] Walter Kaufmann gave the work high praise by stating that "nothing in recent literature, historiography, or political reporting rivals the author's recreation in the first two scenes of the poisoned atmosphere and the variety of the Nazi characters in and around Berlin."[22]

The aspect of the play which has drawn the most heated attention is the portrayal of Pope Pius XII.

Putting the Vicar of Christ in a drama was guaranteed to invoke reaction.[23] Pius is made a fool, a possible position for a historian, writes Walter Kerr, but
not for a dramatist.[24] John Simon complains that the
Pope is merely a caricature,[25] Stanley Kauffman
feels that he is portrayed with facile mockery,[26]
while others protest the Pope is less a person on
stage than an institution.[27]

But there are differing views. Walter Kaufmann
treats Pius as an understandable character, a man
who had a choice, didn't make it, and therefore is
not a tragic figure.[28] Hochhuth himself insists that
"To attribute tragic stature to Pius XII is blasphemy."[29] By such, Pius is seen as a foil for Ricardo,[30] which implies something about the meaning
of the play which I will come to shortly.

The last survey to be made here concerning the
drama as literature is how other characters are understood. Ricardo is called, on the one hand, "shrilly
antipapal" by a critic writing from London,[31] while
on the other hand he is seen as the reason this play is
the only recent example of a major religious drama.[32]
The representation of Kurt Gerstein, that amazing
Nazi figure who risked everything to frustrate the
murderous policy of the Nazis, is labelled a weakly
drawn character by Brustein, who saw the Pope
similarly.[33]

Thus we see the gamut of critical reactions.
While I have studied *The Deputy* as literature some-
what less attentively than I have as history, permit
me, as a teacher of drama history, to share some of
my own conclusions. First, this is not a play about
the cowardice or weakness or evil of a pope; it is the
tragedy of a heroic priest who engaged in a Prom-
ethean disobedience and paid with his life. I deliberately set aside the question of whether or not a genre
titled Christian tragedy is possible. Christians

would have to believe that, given the circumstances of the play, in being martyred Ricardo Fontana saved his soul. I will not pursue this here; suffice it to say that Walter Kaufmann does address the subject and concludes that this play may be the *only* modern Christian tragedy.[34]

To continue my own observations, the subject of this play is not a papal assault. It is, rather, the story of Father Ricardo's martyrdom. Pius appears in one scene covering twenty-seven pages, less than 11 percent of the printed text. That Pius is presented as an institution rather than as a person is credible. When a person changes his own personal pronoun from "I" to "We" it is very difficult to continue to regard him as an individual. This immediate development in the self-referent is not merely a semantic change. When someone is chosen as "The Pope" he instantly accumulates the accoutrements of and the identifications with the institution of the papacy. The taking of a new name, invariably the name of a predecessor after which a number is affixed, certainly adds to this. In *The Deputy*, Pius XII clearly has to stand for an institution. From Hochhuth's point of view the Jews did not suffer because of just one man, Pacelli-become-Pius. The history of Christian anti-Judaism is embodied in the institution represented by the symbol of the pope. That is, as I understand the play, the reason why the playwright does not try to examine the *why* of Pius' silence in the face of monumental crimes. To probe into what motivates Pius would be to treat him as an individual, which is not Hochhuth's purpose here. What we are meant to comprehend is the Bonhoefferian response of the hero Ricardo Fontana who was patterned after a real person, Provost Bernhard Lichtenberg of St. Hedwig's Cathedral in Berlin.

My greatest difficulty with the work, aside from

its length (as far as staging goes), is with the character of the Doctor. He is the most thorough render-
ing of absolute evil since Iago and I fail to see his
motivation as convincing. Even if we believe that
there are such people in the world, in drama and/or
fiction, their reasons for acting the way that they do
have to satisfy us. Additionally, I find some of the
dialogue awkward; the use of tag or identification
lines too obvious on occasion; a scene in which the
audience is supposed to notice an author's name on
a book cover is impossible[35]; the coincidence of
Gerstein running into a Jew (Jacobson) whom he had
"saved" earlier in the play is too pat[36]; Pius' concern
for power plants and railroad terminals instead of for
people is too hyperbolic for effect[37]; and the Cardinal is rather poorly drawn I think.[38] Frankly, ex-
cept for its place in theater history this is not a
drama which I am anxious to see. In book form I find
it challenging and compelling. And I must agree
with Richard Gilman who, while not an admirer of
the drama, wrote: "The real value of Hochhuth's
play is precisely that it can force us back into history, into the intricacies of the relationship between
spirit and aggrieved body, between personal responsibility and institutional indifference."[39]

This brings us to a consideration of the historical
aspects of *The Deputy*. Here we will have to focus
on Pius XII and the Vatican's response to the Holocaust. Hochhuth stresses that in his hand "there is
no imputation that Pius XII and his clergy had antisemitic feelings."[40] I do not know if that is a true
reflection of the thought of Hochhuth the historian
or rather Hochhuth the playwright. After years of
study on this subject I have come to a different conclusion. I cannot even rank Pius among the luke-
warm regarding his Holocaust *in*activity, unwillingness or inability to get involved. In fact, it is

with the fear of judgment *on myself* that I must say that, at least as an institution as the Pope is portrayed in *The Deputy*, and after learning new facts which Hochhuth could not have known when he wrote his drama, the Pope and his Church, my Church, are deeply guilty of antisemitism.

Permit me to continue this sad commentary with a quotation from Francois Mauriac, a Catholic novelist who later won a Nobel Prize for literature:

> We have not yet had the consolation of hearing Simon Peter's successor clearly and sharply condemning, without a trace of tactful circumlocution, the crucifixion of these countless "brothers of Christ." One day during the occupation I asked Cardinal Suhard, who worked so hard for them behind the scenes, to "order us to pray for the Jews"; and he threw up his arms. No doubt the occupying forces were able to bring irresistible pressure to bear, no doubt the silence of the Pope and his Cardinals was a most terrible duty; the important thing being to avoid even worse misfortunes. Nevertheless a crime of such magnitude falls in no small measure to the responsibility of those witnesses who never cried out against it—whatever the reason for their silence.[41]

The Pope during World War II failed to act as a Christian regarding the persecution of Jews. Millions of others failed as well. As the Catholic historian and Viennese theater director Friedrich Heer put it: "The preconditions for Hitler's 'solution' of the Jewish question were, on the one hand, a thousand-year Christian, and also Catholic antisemitism, and in the 19th and 20th centuries a close alliance between leading churchmen and authoritarian, totalitarian, Fascist men and powers." Heer goes on to write about papal alliances with the Czars to whom the Vatican sacrificed Poland, about the Pope's Concordat with Nazi Germany which actually gave a much needed legitimacy to the Hitler

government, and Pius' agreements with Franco and
Mussolini as well. Heer then notes that "The many
thousands of sheets of paper which constitute the
encyclicals, addresses and radio messages of Pope
Pius XII contain no reference to the Jews—nor to the
thousands of Orthodox Serbs murdered by the Catholic Croats."[42]

But let me give an illustration which may be even
more painful. It deals with an encyclical letter written for Pope Pius XI, the war pope's predecessor, by
an American Jesuit, John LaFarge. At Pius XI's request, LaFarge authored a document condemning
fascism and antisemitism. Just before that letter was
to be issued, Pius XI died. When Pius XII succeeded
to the Chair of Peter, he issued an encyclical letter
under the same title as LaFarge's—with all of the
references to antisemitism deleted.[43]

Would the encyclical have done any good? That,
of course, is the wrong question. The moral center of
Catholicism was obligated to make a moral statement. It did not. But we do have examples to indicate that such a major statement from the head of
the Roman Church could have had some effect. The
most heartening example is the reaction of religious
leaders to the Nazi euthanasia program. German
doctors and SS troops murdered some fifty thousand
retarded, crippled, aged, and insane people who were
regarded as burdens to society. Protestants and Catholics, with church officials in the vanguard, protested to such a degree that the Nazis abandoned
that program, at least as policy.[44] This leads us to
wonder what an encyclical opposed to antisemitism
might have achieved. What would the excommunication of Adolf Hitler, who when he died was still on
the tax rolls of the Catholic Church, have achieved?
And placing Germany under a papal interdict would
have to have had an enormous impact. There was

precedent for such action. Pope Pius VII excommunicated the supporters of Napoleon[45] and Pius XII himself, in 1949, excommunicated Communists from the Church, but never Nazis.[46] Yet, no such action was ever threatened.

During the Holocaust, the Pope opted for silence. Late in the war, a correspondent reports, when Pius was asked why he did not speak out on the persecution of the Jews, we are told that the Pontiff replied with the following words: "Dear friend, do not forget that millions of Catholics serve in the German armies. Shall I bring them into conflicts of conscience?"[47]

Yet, the Vatican did break its silence a number of times. It reacted against Russia's invasion of Finland[48] and Pius expressed concern over the German invasions of Holland, Belgium and Luxembourg.[49] He even wrote to Roosevelt for protection from possible Allied bombing of Rome.[50]

Perhaps the most effective critic of the Vatican's overall inactivity concerning Jews is Father John F. Morley of the Department of Religious Studies at Seton Hall University. His book, *Vatican Diplomacy and the Jews During the Holocaust 1939–1943*,[51] is a treasure of research and analysis on the subject. He concludes that he does not find Pius XII to have been motivated by malevolence or anti-semitism but that he was locked into certain ecclesiastical and personal concepts from which he could not break free.[52] Morely writes that Vatican diplomacy failed the Jews by not doing all that it could have on their behalf and thereby betrayed itself as well. "The nuncios, the secretary of state, and, most of all, the Pope share responsibility for this dual failure."[53]

Morley notes that diplomacy was the principal instrument used by the Vatican during the Second

World War period to exert moral authority and examines this diplomacy.[54] He finds Vatican diplomacy woefully and seriously flawed in many ways. For example, Morley found that while some nuncios complained about Nazi racial laws as they affected baptized Jews, they did not attack the basic injustice of such legislation. "In fact, on the contrary, some of them felt that certain aspects of the anti-Jewish legislation would be beneficial in minimizing Jewish influence in countries where it was considered harmful to Christian society."[55] Some Church officers even saw Jewish conversions to Catholicism at this time, while perhaps motivated by attempts to escape persecution, as the result of divine grace resulting from heavenly approval of Nazi racial policies.[56] We ought not be surprised, then, at the words contained in a statement issued by the Church's Commissariat for Jewish Affairs in 1941: ". . . from information obtained from the most authoritative sources, there is nothing in the legislation worked out for the protection of France from Jewish influence which is in opposition to Church doctrine."[57] That the Holocaust was seen as a divine chastisement of Jews and as a means to bring Jews to the Catholic faith is a sign of the theological atmosphere pervading the Church.[58]

It is not difficult to understand, therefore, that when the Vatican did choose at certain times to speak out on behalf of Jews, however weakly, the concern was primarily and almost exclusively for baptized Jews.[59] (It should be indicated that baptized Jews were in a unique position during the Nazi period because they were cut off from support of aid by *Jewish* relief organizations[60] and no doubt suffered from the lack of sustenance which a community might offer—and this may be seen as a scandal in its own right.)

Another reason given for the Vatican's unwillingness to aid the efforts of some Jews for resettlement was the fear of Jewish emigration to Palestine. The Pope's personally appointed Secretary of State, Cardinal Luigi Maglioni (who must share a great deal of the blame for Vatican policies during this period), was afraid that Jewish control of the Holy Land would limit Catholicism's historical rights over Christian shrines. Maglioni urged that a home territory for Jews be found elsewhere than the Middle East, somewhere "which would be better suited for that purpose, while Palestine, under a Jewish majority, would give rise to new and grave international problems, would displease Catholics throughout the entire world, would provoke the justifiable protest of the Holy See, and would badly correspond to the charitable concern that the same Holy See has had and continues to have for the Jews."[61] Or, as one of Maglioni's two chief assistants, Msgr. Domenico Tardini, so succinctly put it: "And the question of the Holy Places? Palestine is by this time more sacred for Catholics than . . .for Jews."[62]

It would be false to give the impression that the Vatican was totally silent about the plight of Jews in Europe under Hitler. While the number (although relatively small) of priests who interceded on behalf of Jews in one way or another did so without direction or leadership from Rome, there was some activity emanating from the official Church. That such activity was not ineffectual may be witnessed to by the fact that Rome's chief rabbi, Israel Zolli, converted to Catholicism and took the Pope's first name for his own at baptism.[63] (Other Jews approved Pius' strategy of not condemning Nazi policies against them.)[64] There is no question of papal approval of the hiding of some four thousand Roman Jews in monasteries and religious houses in the Eter-

nal City[65] and Pius made money available to Jews
fleeing the invaders.[66]

Yet the overall judgment must be a negative one,
given the totality of evidence available to us, much of
which Rolf Hochhuth could not have known. Xavier
Vallat, the commissioner for Jewish affairs at Vichy,
stated that no reaction to anti-Jewish legislation
from either the French episcopate or the Vatican was
taken by him as a sign of consent.[67] The French
ambassador admitted that he viewed this as a historical pattern evident in Church practices.[68] The Vatican protested the original racial laws as promulgated
in Slovakia, not because of their effects on Jews but
rather because they threatened the rights of the
Church.[69] When the Vatican did speak out more
strongly the outcome of the war had been virtually
decided.[70] The Pope did pronounce with finality, as
one of his defenders has written, but the fact is the
words came on March 18, 1945, just shortly before
the war's end![71]

Secretary of State Maglioni, with whom the Pope
was in daily contact, delayed even minimal protest
because he apparently feared being duped by Allied
propaganda,[72] despite the overwhelming proof of
what Germans and others were doing to Jews. When
presented with evidence, Maglioni seemed more
concerned with the source of the information at
hand[73] than with the persecutions themselves.

The Catholic Church has been blamed not only
for an ongoing, abhorrent attitude toward Jews, but
also for a fixation on its own temporal security.[74]
Hochhuth puts it one way in his play when the Cardinal faults Ricardo for being an idealist. It's as if
this character does not take Jesus very seriously
when he says, "In the end the idealist always spills
blood in the delusion that he is doing good—*more*
blood than any realist."[75] In his historical note to

his play, Hochhuth refers to an article in *Der Spiegel* which claimed that the Jesuits made profits from both sides in the war and that the Vatican is the largest stockholder in the world[76]—this long before the recent bank scandal, long before the rumors current in Rome that Pope John Paul I was poisoned because of his interest in cleaning up that economic mess.

What are we to conclude from the mass of data and commentaries? One writer felt compelled to observe that "not a single German bishop went to his martyrdom, and Hitler, the fascist beast, did not die excommunicated."[77] Guenter Lewy has shown how the official Jesuit publication, *Civilta Cattolica*, "noted with regret that the anti-Semitism of the Nazis 'did not stem from the religious convictions nor the Christian conscience . . . , but from . . . their desire to upset the order of religion and society.' The *Civilta Cattolica* added that, 'we could understand them, or even praise them, if their policy were restricted within acceptable bounds of defense against the Jewish organizations and institutions.'"[78]

There have been pieces written in support of Pope Pius XII and they need to be noticed. However, in general, they are necessarily inadequate. A pamphlet by Jesuit Father Robert A. Graham is embarrassing in its attempted defense. Published by the Catholic League in this country, it is a work without footnote references and contains sentences like this: "The iron law of war left little room for the work of any would-be Good Samaritans."[79] Graham's presentation of Archbishop Cesare Orsenigo is curious. He holds up Orsenigo as a man devoted to justice,[80] the same man whom the bishop of Berlin, Konrad von Preysing (to whom Pius XII wrote more letters between 1939 and 1944 than to any other prelate),[81] complained to the Pope because, Preysing lamented,

Orsenigo has a greater loyalty to the Gestapo than to fellow Catholics.[82] Elsewhere, Father Graham, in defending the Pope, observed that Jesus himself "didn't go forth in a general career of denouncing every evil wherever he found it."[83] And Graham then adds that "I find that his [Hochhuth's] image of the papacy is exactly that which I read in Communist literature against the Vatican."[84]

Cardinal Giovanni Batista Montini, before he became Pope Paul VI, reacted quite negatively to the message of *The Deputy*, a play he admitted to not having seen. Montini's faint rejoinder is replete with phrases like "I cannot myself conceive how anyone . . . " and "I could cite a host of particular facts . . . " which he then does not do.[85] What Montini fails to mention in his piece is that, along with the previously named Domenico Tardini, he was the chief assistant to Vatican Secretary of State Maglioni and so was himself implicitly criticized whenever the Pope and Vatican were for anti-Judaic silence. Furthermore, as Hochhuth wrote in response to an anonymous critic's views in London's *Times Literary Supplement*, "the attitude of Under-Secretary of State Montini to the deportations of the Roman Jews was made clear only after discussions on the subject with Hitler's diplomatic representative to the Vatican at the time."[86] Such procedures cast doubt on Montini's value as a commentator on the whole situation.

Charges and responses have been raised concerning the Vatican's relations with the Jews during the Third Reich. It might not be out of order to summarize them briefly. It is said that Pius XII was unmoved by the plight of the Jews; the response is that the Pope condemned evil generally, not specifically. Pius did not abrogate the Concordat with Germany. This was an error some claim; this protected the churches in Nazi territories is the other view. When Jews and even Catholics were deported from Rome, Pius remained silent is a charge; protests had proven ineffective so the Pope worked behind the scenes is the answer to that. Open protest, as done by Church officials in Hungary, Czechoslovakia and Rumania, would have been helpful assert certain historians; regional governments could be dealt with but Hitler could not has been the reply. The Vatican failed to point out the evils of antisemitism in Germany is another charge to which the response is that Rome complained as early as 1933 only to be ignored by Hitler. People have written that the Pope feared Communism so much that he favored Hitler as a lesser evil, although some insist this is not true. The differences in assessing papal action and inaction can be seen from this short review.[87]

The overwhelming evidence, however, favors those who have been critical of the papacy regarding the Holocaust, its roots and, a topic not to be gone into here, the post-Holocaust era of Jewish-Christian relations. The failure to excommunicate, to interdict, to bear witness, to demand a total Catholic response, and, yes, the failure by the Vatican to this day to recognize the existence of the State of Israel, have had tragic results.

Notes

1. Catharine Hughes, *Plays, Politics, and Polemics* (New York: Drama Book Specialists, 1973), p. 127. Ms. Hughes quotes Eric Bentley as saying that the reaction to *The Deputy* is "almost certainly the largest storm ever raised by a play in the whole history of the drama."

2. Walter Kaufmann, *Tragedy and Philosophy* (Garden City, N.Y.: Doubleday, 1968), pp. 329–30 n. 13.

3. Ibid., pp. 329–31.

4. Friedrich Heer, "The Need for Confession," *Commonweal*, Feb. 28, 1964, p. 657.

5. This is the estimate of Hughes, p. 128.

6. Kaufmann, *Tragedy*, p. 323, notes that this length compares to an Aeschylean trilogy plus satyr play and further says this is not much longer than *Lear*, a Sophoclean tragedy or Shaw's *Man and Superman*.

7. John Simon, *Singularities* (New York: Random House, 1975), p. 171. See also Robert Brustein, *Seasons of Discontent* (New York: Simon and Schuster, 1965), p. 206, where he says the New York version is "beneath discussion."

8. Alfred Kazin, "The Deputy," *New York Review of Books*, Mar. 19, 1965, p. 3.

9. Walter Kerr, *Thirty Plays Hath November* (New York: Simon and Schuster, 1969), p. 204.

10. Brustein, p. 204.

11. Susan Sontag, *Against Interpretation* (New York: Farrar, Straus & Giroux, 1966), p. 128.

12. Eric Bentley, *The Theatre of Commitment* (New York: Atheneum, 1967), pp. 210, 217.

13. Brustein, pp. 205–6.

14. Stanley Kaufmann, *Persons of the Drama* (New York: Harper & Row, 1976), p. 162.

15. Hughes, p. 136.

16. Sontag, p. 125.

17. Ibid.

18. Ibid., p. 128.

19. Brustein, p. 207.

20. Harold E. Fey, "*The Deputy* Controversy," *Christian Century*, Apr. 22, 1964, p. 508.

21. Simon, p. 171.

22. Kaufmann, *Tragedy*, p. 327.

23. Bentley agrees, p. 207.

24. Kerr, p. 89.

25. Simon, p. 168.

26. Kaufmann, *Persons*, p. 161.

27. Ewart E. Turner, "No Letup for *Der Stellvertretter*," *Christian Century*, Oct. 16, 1963, p. 1269.

28. Kaufmann, *Tragedy*, p. 330 n. 13.

29. Rolf Hochhuth, "Letters to the Editor," *Times Literary Supplement*, Oct. 11, 1963, p. 812.

30. Kaufmann, *Tragedy*, p. 326.

31. Mary Zavada, "Hochhuth in London," *America*, Jan. 25, 1964, p. 140.

32. Simon, p. 170.

33. Brustein, p. 206.

34. See W. Kaufmann's discussion, *Tragedy*, pp. 329–31.

35. Rolf Hochhuth, *The Deputy* (New York: Grove Press, 1964), p. 251.

36. Ibid., p. 266.

37. Ibid., p. 195.

38. It is very difficult to comprehend how such a "character" could have risen in church politics.

39. Richard Gilman, *Common and Uncommon Masks* (New York: Random House, 1971), p. 166.

40. Hochhuth, *The Deputy*, p. 331.

41. Quoted after the preface in *The Deputy*.

42. Heer, p. 658.

43. Harry James Cargas, *A Christian Response to the Holocaust* (Denver: Stonehenge, 1981), pp. 181–83.

44. Nora Levin, *The Holocaust* (New York: Schocken, 1973), pp. 301–16.

45. Andre Gisselbrecht, "A Young Man's Polemic Against Whom?" in *The Deputy Reader*, edited by Dolores Barracano Schmidt and Earl Robert Schmidt (Chicago: Scott, Foresman, 1965), p. 195.

46. Kaufmann, *Tragedy* p. 326.

47. Quoted in Levin, p. 691.

48. Sontag, p. 130.

49. Guenter Lewy, "Pius XII, the Jews and the German Catholic Church," *Commentary*, Feb., 1964, p. 33.

50. Hochhuth, "Letters," p. 812.

51. John R Morley, *Vatican Diplomacy and the Jews During the Holocaust 1939–1943* (New York: KTAV, 1980).

52. Ibid., p. 209.

53. Ibid.

54. Ibid., p. 6.

55. Ibid., p. 198.

56. Ibid., p. 197.

57. Ibid., p. 53.

58. Ibid., p. 30.

59. Ibid., p. 21.

60. Ibid., p. 18.

61. Ibid., p. 93.

62. Ibid., p. 92.

63. Hughes, pp. 135–36.

64. Joseph Lichten, "A Jewish Defense," *Commonweal*, Feb. 28, 1964, p. 661.

65. Lewy, p. 31.

66. Ibid.

67. Morley, pp. 50–51.

68. Ibid., p. 51.

69. Ibid., p. 74.

70. Ibid., pp. 100–101.

71. Michel Roquet, "Le Catholique Bafoue" *Le Figaro*, Dec. 19, 1963, p. 6; in Schmidt and Schmidt, p. 194.

72. Morley, p. 203.

73. Ibid., p. 109.

74. Emile Capouya, "Cry Against a Decision of Silence," *Saturday Review*, Mar. 21, 1964, p. 41.

75. Hochhuth, *The Deputy*, p. 115.

76. Ibid., p. 350. (See the playwright's use of this information in *The Deputy*, p. 105.)

77. Gisselbrecht, quoted in Schmidt and Schmidt, p. 195.

78. Lewy, p. 30.

79. Robert A Graham, "Pius XII's Defense of Jews and Others: 1944–45" (Milwaukee: Catholic League for Religious and Civil Rights, n.d.), p. 9.

80. Ibid., p. 10.

81. Morley, p. 105.

82. Ibid.

83. In Schmidt and Schmidt, p. 213.

84. Ibid., p. 214.

85. Pope Paul VI, "Letter from Pope Paul VI," *Commonweal*, Feb. 28, 1964, p. 652.

86. Hochhuth, "Letters," p. 812.

87. See Schmidt and Schmidt, pp. 177–79.

My Papal Encyclical

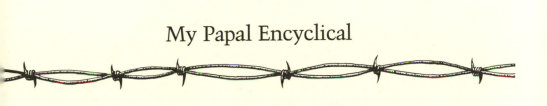

For over two decades now I have written and spoken of the need for the official Catholic Church to make a serious gesture of repentance concerning the role of many Catholics in the overwhelming Sin of the Holocaust and of the hierarchy's responsibility in that crime. For reasons stated in this piece, an encyclical letter would be an appropriate, albeit late manifestation of the acknowledgement of guilt concerning the Shoah. Since nothing approaching the kind of proclamation I feel necessary has been promulgated, I took it upon myself to write a suggested letter for the Pope to all of the faithful, to all the world. It is found in *Methodology in the Academic Teaching of the Holocaust* (Zev Garber, ed., University Press of America, 1988) and is dedicated to the memory of Terrence Des Pres, whose presence is missed but whose beacon is not dimmed.

The Roman Catholic Church is not so structured that everything is decided at the papal level and then disseminated downward for implementation. While it is not a democratic institution, for the faithful masses to influence the hierarchy is not without certain precedents. The dogma of the Assumption of the Virgin Mary bodily into heaven is an example of a belief so popular that Vatican officials could not ignore it—they examined it, validated it, and made it a tenet of faith for members of its Church.

One cannot say that the majority of Catholics today is clamoring for a reconciliation with Jews, a
reconciliation which must acknowledge the atrocities committed against Jews by Christians over the
centuries, and in particular those injuries done
against Jews in World War II known as having made
up the Holocaust. But regardless of the lack of wide-
spread fervor on this subject, its truth remains.
Many Catholics sinned grievously in their actions
and in their silence against Jews. The division
caused between Catholics (and other Christians) and
Jews during World War II may be irreparable. In one
sense, that decision must be left up to the Jews, the
victims. Nevertheless, it is morally necessary that
we Christians—the persecutors—make strong and
sincere attempts at harmonizing relationships with
Jews through repentance for our continued historical behavior in regard to them.

Hence it would be fitting if, since the Catholic
hierarchy does not appear to be making enough significant steps in this area, the faithful demanded
action. In 1938, a papal encyclical condemning antisemitism was commissioned, was written by the
American Jesuit John LaFarge, but was never promulgated. Now, over a generation after the Holocaust,
where millions of people were systematically put to
death, where some six million were Jews, and where
one million of these victims were children, it is time
that we required the publication of an up-to-date
encyclical concerning the vital issue of Catholic-
Jewish relationships.

Since encyclical letters are usually drafted for
popes by others who are specialists in the subjects of
each epistle, it may not be without value for me to
here submit a suggested draft of such a letter on this
topic. This is not offered in the sense of satire, once
removed, or, I hope, from arrogance or an attitude of

presumptuousness. Rather, it is written in hope: hope that other members of my Church agree on the need for such a document, and hope that Jewish women and men throughout the world can believe in the sincerity of approach that some of us Christians have when we profess our love for them, or sorrow for certain past misdeeds and our firm purpose of amendment regarding our future relations with Jews.

A papal encyclical is usually known by the first two words of the letter, hence these words are carefully chosen. I would like this suggested work to begin with words which are very descriptive of the purpose of the letter:

Seeking reconciliation with Jews throughout the world because we are mindful of the many centuries of pain caused them by persons who called themselves good Christians, we address this document to men and women of goodwill everywhere, but especially to Catholics who must be concerned over the evils done to the Jews by their coreligionists. We likewise address this letter to our Jewish brothers and sisters indirectly in the hope that they may understand that our sincerity to and love for them is the motivating force of this encyclical.

Too often the relationship between Christians and Jews has been in the form of persecutor and persecuted, of torturer and tortured, of murderer and victim. Whether we remember such historical periods as the Crusades, the Inquisition, pogroms, or the Holocaust, we Christians must ever acknowledge our guilt in the eyes of others and in the eyes of God for our treatment of those we have also recognized as being among His Chosen People.

Perhaps because it is closest to us in time of all the major persecutions about which we here write, and certainly because of the magnitude of the tragedy, we must particularly regret and make reparation in whatever ways possible for our role in the crime of the Holocaust. It is appropriate that we do this as a group, as a Mystical Body in which we all participate as Christians. If the virtues done by Christians, past and present, form a kind of spiritual reservoir upon which the world Christian community draws for moral sustenance, then we must also admit that the sins of Christians are not without effect on us as well. Indeed contemporary psychology seems to prove that nothing which has ever happened or been thought can ever be lost, can ever be without some influence, however small. In the case of the Holocaust, we cannot honestly speak of small effects. The word *Holocaust* stands for that collection of enormous evils which were perpetrated against helpless, defenseless, guiltless Jews and others—we emphasize again that the vast majority of the perpetrators was Christian.

With the foregoing ever present in our minds, then, let us consider actions which we may take toward reconciling Christians with Jews. We must do this following the examples of Christians whose devotion to the entirety of humanity during the Holocaust exemplifies the finest in the followers of Christ: men and women like Franz Jagersdatter, Marion Pritchard, Dietrich Bonhoeffer, Pope John XXIII, Alfred Delp, Martin Niemoeller, Rufino Niccacci and the others (also, too few) who followed the call of Christianity to its logical end in heroism.

As a sign of our total commitment to reconciliation through acknowledgment of our errors, then, we begin by the ecclesiastical powers vested in us, by belatedly excommunicating Adolf Hitler from the Catholic Church. Excommunication is a punishment for the living and since Hitler is dead it may seem meaningless to make this public pronouncement. We do not do so to perform a meaningless act. We do so in order to indicate to our Jewish brothers and sisters that we regret this not having been done in the 1930s, that Hitler was guilty of unspeakable crimes against humanity against which the Church should not have been silent, and we do so as a warning to all those who would today espouse Hitler's teachings opposed to the Jews. Such teachings are anathema and any who support them are guilty of grave sin. It must not be overlooked that this is the first time in the history of our Church that excommunication has been pronounced on a dead person. We do so because of the seriousness of his crimes and as an admission that our silence during his lifetime may itself have been contributory to these crimes.

We urge the Christian clergy throughout the world to emphasize the import of such action. Ideally, they would use this as a starting point for thoughtful, prayerful homilies on the meaning of the Holocaust for Christianity. For us, perhaps even more than for the Jews, the Holocaust is an enormous tragedy. How could we have stood by and watched it take place? How could we have participated in this monumental sin? Some have thought that the Holocaust marks the end of Christianity. It is our prayer that from the ashes of the fires at Dachau, Bergen-Belsen, Auschwitz, and other murderous locations we will see an unparalleled resurrection, as it were, of a truly meaningful Christianity which will touch all of our hearts and be evident for having done so to all people of all faiths everywhere and for all time to come.

If the homilies on the Holocaust are to be effective, they will have to admit to errors in the works of our teachers concerning the Jews. St. John Chrysostom was wrong in saying that God hates the

Jews and always hated them. St. Justin was wrong
when he said that the Jews had been made to suffer
because they killed Christ. St. Cyprian was wrong
when he said that the peoplehood of the Jews has
been cancelled. St. Jerome was wrong when he spoke
of the Jews as serpents, St. Abrogard was wrong to
write a treatise on the superstitions of Jews. Many,
far too many, such statements must be abjured.
Whole theologies have been built on their foundation and since the foundation has proven false, the
structure must be seen as uninhabitable.

In addition to the above, we proclaim in this letter that an annual memorial service for Jewish victims of the Holocaust be instituted in the liturgical
calendar with comparable national, diocesan and
parish programs to support the material. A mass
should be said for this purpose on the Sabbath of
each year closest to the day the Jews have chosen as
the international day of remembrance of the Holocaust, *Yom Hashoah*.

We now turn to the sacred scriptures themselves
to examine if they have, in some way, contributed to
the persecution of Jews. By this we do not in any
way imply the inauthenticity of the Christian Bible.
Rather, we raise questions about the interpretations
of holy writ which have caused so much grief. To
question is not to judge. We must keep in mind that
we have nothing to fear from truth. Rather, we welcome continual theological study of scriptures, as
the Church has practiced since its beginning. This
includes study of the very difficult problems as well
as those which cause less difficulty. Yes, even less
embarrassment we ought to say. The subject of
Christian-Jewish relations, as influenced by our
scriptures, is one which requires deep, prayerful,
sensitive and continued probing.

Preliminary to such examinations, we must acknowledge that the Christian terminology for the scriptures is not conducive to bettering Jewish-Christian harmony. The terms Old Testament and New Testament are seen as insulting to some Jews and have even been considered as evidence of Christian arrogance. It would be extremely problematical to expect that our sincere and prayer-laden approaches to reconciliation with Jews could be deeply effective if the very core of our spiritual rootedness, the scriptures, were named in a way so as to divide us. Therefore we urge Catholic theologians, religious and the laity to abandon the terms Old Testament and New Testament in favor of more universally accepted names. The title "Hebrew Scriptures" cannot be applied to what is now known as the Old Testament since that body contains work which is outside the traditional Jewish canon. Thus the simple division of Hebrew scriptures and Christian scriptures would be inaccurate. By way of suggestion, but not insistence—theologians will do well to turn their attention to this area of nomenclature—we might consider calling the chronologically earlier portion of the Bible "Inherited Testament" with all of the respect to our religious forebears which that phrase implies, and the latter portion "Institutional Testament" with the recognition of the Church's role in solely establishing this canon being thus acknowledged. We reiterate, however, that we do not insist on these terms but rather suggest them as at least beginning points for theologians to consider.

All of this implies, of course, the essential Jewishness of Christianity. The Church must be proud of its heritage and this glory is to be ever regarded, publicly in liturgical celebrations and homilies as well as in the utterances and writings of Christians,

and privately in the hearts of all Christians who will
thus be fully aware that the persecution of Jews, as
with the persecution of all persons, is reprehensible
to God. By insisting on the basic Jewish roots of
Christianity we will also readily recognize that the
Jewish Nazarene worshipped by Christians as the
Son of God is not to be regarded as a being who
divides Christians and Jews but as a link between us.
It is fitting that on this topic we recognize the
wisdom of a document written in the United States
under the ecumenical sponsorship of the Commission on Faith and Order of the National Council of
Churches and the Secretariat for Catholic-Jewish Relations of the National Conference for Catholic
Bishops. It reads in part: "The Church of Christ is
rooted in the life of the people of Israel. We Christians
look upon Abraham as our spiritual ancestor and
father of our faith. . . . The ministry of Jesus and the
life of the early Christian community were thor-
oughly rooted in the Judaism of their day, particularly in the teachings of the Pharisees. The Christian
Church is still sustained by the living faith of the
patriarchs and prophets, kings and priests, scribes
and rabbis, and the people whom God chose for his
own. Christ is the link . . . enabling the Gentiles to
be numbered among Abraham's 'offspring' and therefore fellow-heirs with the Jews according to God's
promise. It is a tragedy of history that Jesus, our bond
of unity with the Jews, has all too often become a
symbol and source of division and bitterness because
of human weakness and pride." These words are elo-
quently written and reflect precisely the instruction
which is meant here. It is a betrayal of the mission of
Jesus Christ to regard him as divisive rather than
unitive among human beings, and particularly
among Christians and Jews.

With this document we wish not only to admonish and encourage but to set an example by taking action as well. Our proclamation of the excommunication of Adolf Hitler, our revision of the liturgical calendar to include a Holocaust memorial, are steps in this direction. In addition to these, we now declare that the Vatican historical archives, up to the year 1970, are hereby opened to qualified scholars throughout the world. Secrecy is unnecessary and even harmful regarding the events leading up to and transpiring both during and after World War II. If we are sincere about reconciling ourselves with our Jewish brothers and sisters, then we must admit where we have been weak, where we have been wrong, where we have sinned against them. The Vatican archives contain much material which will shed light on these times. We must examine our mistakes so that we will learn from them and not be condemned to repeat them ever. Something else will happen, also, when the archives are studied. The names and acts of a large number of heroic Christians will be brought to public attention. While our great errors are hidden in the archives, so also are our virtuous people and works who resisted the implementation of Nazi policies in saintly fashion. We do a disservice to these good people in not allowing their stories to be told and opening the archives of the Vatican will undoubtedly foster the dissemination of knowledge of their courage. We instruct the opening of the Vatican archives, up through December 31, 1969, immediately. We must hide nothing. We must admit, where admitting is necessary, we may take pride where that is justifiable.

There is another way we must be open, as well, and that is in the studying of the true meaning of Judaism. If we regard the Jewish religion only as embodying truths as a forerunner of Christianity, we can never fully understand what the religion means to its followers. Care is to be taken that we as Christians do not regard Judaism simplistically from a supercessionist point of view. It is wholly arrogant to profess that Judaism has existed solely as a predecessor to Christianity, meant only to be fulfilled in Christianity. Jews today comprise a body that we regard as God's Chosen People just as they did over two thousand years ago. Their uniqueness in this way should cause us to revere, admire, love and attempt to understand them more completely. Therefore, with this encyclical, we urge very strongly that where possible, at Catholic colleges and universities throughout the world, chairs of Judaic studies be established for the purpose of teaching us about Jews and their religion. Nor ought we fail to mention that such positions would be more appropriately filled by Jewish scholars, generally speaking, than by Christian scholars. This appears self-evident yet frequently the truths of Judaism are so often taught on Christian campuses by non-Jews. In some cases the results have been other than we here intend with this instruction. Where Jewish and Christian traditions come in apparent conflict, these differences must be recognized and discussed. However, they must always be discussed in an atmosphere of charity, mutual respect and a fervent desire only to pursue the truth.

In addition, we urge authorities in Catholic high schools and elementary schools to make extraordinary efforts to bring their pupils in touch with the true Judaism and with Jews in the community. Sadly necessary, also, are lessons, on all educational levels, dealing with the Holocaust. Both the failures and virtuous actions of Christians during that period of twentieth-century history are to be taught.

Many of the sins against the Jews which have been committed by Christians are a result of the heavy emphasis on missionizing in which we Christians have been engaged for so long. True missionary efforts are turned inward; all of us who call ourselves Christian need to bear witness to Christ by perfecting our individual, personal lives. To try to convert others while neglecting ourselves is once again to act with sinful arrogance. We may learn from the great work done by the beloved members of the religious of the Congregation of Notre Dame De Sion, founded in France in 1846. Originally established to bring about better understanding between Christians and Jews, and for the conversion of the latter to Christianity, this remarkable religious group has changed its goals since the events of World War II. The emphasis is now on Christian-Jewish dialogue and the insistence is that proselytizing by members of the congregation is to be completely abandoned. If, in fact, we are to expect Jews to trust us when we say that we wish to offer them true friendship, the ulterior motive of conversion must be absent. We urge this attitude on all of the faithful.

We submit this letter to all the world in prayerful humility, on our knees, to express a profound repentance. While addressed to Catholics of the world, it is our prayer that Jews everywhere read this letter and understand our intent. We have attempted simple, straightforward language in an open fashion. Nothing is meant to be hidden; there is no aim at ambiguity of expression. For all sins by Christians against Jews, we are truly sorry. For the future relationship between Christians and Jews, we are hopeful. We do not expect that Jews, who have for so long been victimized by unworthy Christians, will immediately embrace us and fully trust our motives.

The long history that they have endured precludes that. However, we make this beginning, and while it will certainly take a long time for Jewish-Christian relations to reach the point that they should, we do make this beginning. Christians must be patient and not be disappointed if we are not quickly and totally accepted as loving sisters and brothers by the Jews. However, we know that with God's aid and a firm purpose of commitment, we can succeed.

Finally, and without amplification, the Vatican hereby officially extends the offer of full diplomatic relations with the State of Israel.

On Meeting Kurt Waldheim

AN OPEN LETTER TO POPE JOHN PAUL II

The perplexing blunder of Pope John Paul II in meeting
with Austria's Kurt Waldheim and scheduled subsequent
official encounters between the two leaders have troubled
many people and caused papal apologists to look silly trying to explain the pontiff's motives. Their excuses were an
embarrassment. I thought it important that dissenting
Catholic views be aired so I composed this public document, which was distributed in booklet form by the Holocaust Memorial Foundation of Illinois and is dedicated to
my friend Dr. William Kahn, whose energy, whether directed towards work or human relations, is inspiring.

My Brother in Christ,

The cause of my letter is your reception of Kurt
Waldheim. (I am also puzzled by your words of
praise for him when you said that "All of your activity in the course of an international life as a diplo-
mat and foreign minister of your country and also in
your difficult work, full of responsibility, at the
United Nations was always devoted to securing
peace among people.") I am further troubled that
you have scheduled another meeting with Waldheim for June of 1988 in Austria. It seems to me
that your first encounter was nothing less than a
Papal Bitburg, an event which would obviously

cause so much anguish to Jews and Christians—and
I emphasize that it is not Jews alone who are pained
by the official reception of Waldheim; many, many
Christians have been thus hurt and embarrassed—
that another such visit can only compound the harm
done.

First, I ask a question that so many have asked:
Why did you meet with Waldheim? Certainly, I
don't have to remind you what symbols and memory are to the Church. Everyday, all over the world, in
symbol-filled liturgies, the words "Do this in memory of me" are reverently uttered. The spiritual un-
derpinning of the Vatican itself is rooted in symbol
and memory. And Kurt Waldheim is a symbol who
recalls memories of the most bitter of tragedies.
Why did you meet with a man who lied about his
role as a Nazi and who presided over the United
Nations when it voted to equate Zionism with racism? We really see from your many good words that
you are not antisemitic, but where the official
Church is on the question of Jews has long been
called into question, called into question by the actions of the official Church and by some of its members. Is William F. Buckley, who initially came to
your defense on the Waldheim visit, correct in a
later assessment when he wrote that "The word that
comes to mind is that (the pope) has been manipulated, and there are those who don't much like it
when the pope is manipulated"?

Cardinal John O'Conner was forbidden by the
Vatican to meet with top political leaders when he
visited Israel recently. In the context of your wel-
coming Waldheim, this is very curious. An Argen-
tine man who had been imprisoned and tortured by
his government—a Catholic—told me that when
you visited his country, you refused to meet with
mothers and other relatives of that government's

human rights victims and other human rights leaders. You ordered Jesuit Father Robert Drinan, this
great friend of Israel and of the Jewish people, to
surrender his seat in the U.S. House of Representatives while allowing other clergy around the world
to be very involved in politics—Cardinal Jamie Sin
of the Philippines comes to mind as the first of many
examples.

Apologists for your hosting of Waldheim have repeatedly told us that we don't know what went on in
the private half hour meeting that you had. But
that's my point, not theirs. What did you talk about?
There were hints carefully dropped that Waldheim
even might have confessed moral crimes that he
may have committed. That is an unacceptable insin-
uation. The Church has long advocated that public
sinners must repent publicly. The American criminal Al Capone, we were taught, could not have gone
to confession privately on Saturday night and then
gone to Holy communion in public on Sunday because that would have been a source of great scandal. I see a parallel with the Waldheim visit.

The question of forgiveness here is a significant
one. It is my hope that Waldheim will seek the forgiveness of the Church if he sincerely repents and
acknowledges his role as a Nazi and for whatever
other sins he may have a need to confess. Nevertheless, he must seek not only forgiveness according to
the spiritual guidelines of his Church but he must
also beg the forgiveness of those whom he has victimized. Jews cannot understand, nor can many
Christians, how it is that Waldheim can make his
peace within his Church but not with the very people he is accused of harming. As Sister Mary Jo Led-
dy, editor of the *Catholic New Times* in Toronto and
Sister Carol Rittner, director of the Elie Wiesel
Foundation for Humanity and Dr. Eva Fleischner,

advisor to the National Conference of Catholic
Bishops, have written in the *National Catholic Reporter*, "Pope John Paul II gave the world a magnifi-
cent example of forgiveness when he visited Ma-
hmet Ali Agca in prison. The pope, who was the
victim, forgave the one who had wounded him. The
pope, however, did not ask that Agca be released
from prison, from the social consequences of his
wrong."

I do not wish to overemphasize the negative effect
which your meeting with Kurt Waldheim has had on
Jews and many Christians alike. You are, after all, the
representative of a church which, in the Second Vatican Council proceedings, made important strides
toward reconciliation between Catholics—indeed
Christians—and Jews. And this was reinforced with
the publication of *Nostrae Aetate* during your pon-
tificate. As Rabbi Leon Klenicki noted, "In such pro-
gressive interpretations, one can see the positive development of church teaching today." And Jewish
writer Annette Daum has said quite recently, "Revo-
lutionary changes are taking place in Catholic teaching to implement the principles expressed in *Nostrae
Aetate* and subsequent Vatican guidelines, to eliminate antisemitic references, to repudiate the charge,
and to correct misconceptions of the Jews and Judaism." One can only be heartened by such facts. Nor
am I unmindful of your August letter to the spiritual
head of my own Catholic community here is St.
Louis, Archbishop John L. May, President of the National Conference of Catholic Bishops, where you
express your concern for Jewish suffering, particularly in the Shoah. But this is what makes your meeting with Waldheim, particularly the proposed second
encounter, all the more confusing. There is an ambiguity of approach which is difficult for many to com-

prehend. And these are times in Christian-Jewish relations where ambiguity has no place.

The massacre of nearly 6,000,000 Jews during the Holocaust was an extraordinary event, one which requires an extraordinary response. That response has not been made. Acts which are symbolic and effective, dramatic and significant, are imperative. Perhaps the most important single action which the Church can take regarding Jews is to repent for past crimes committed in the name of Christianity by Christians against the Jews. Leviticus says, "And you shall confess your sins and those of your fathers." That is in the spirit of Jesus, the Jew, as well. As a Catholic novelist, Mary Gordon, has written: "Grave offenses have been committed against Jews by the Catholic Church. There is no reason for Jews to trust or forgive the church until it has acknowledged the depths of its offenses." Add to this A.M. Rosenthal's words regarding the Waldheim affair: "Popes do not often apologize, but a word of regret from John Paul II would soothe millions of Jewish hearts." And I might add, "Christian hearts as well."

What is the difficulty in saying that we are sorry? Nobody is blaming you or me for the atrocities of history. But they become our atrocities if we do not repudiate them. I am not responsible for the pogroms that litter European history; nor for the ghettoization of Jews throughout the Christian West; nor for the kidnapping of Jewish babies in order to baptize them and keep them from their Jewish parents in the Middle Ages; nor for the restriction of Jews from certain professions; nor for the forcing of Jews to wear humiliating clothing so that they would be distinguished from Christians. I did not participate in expropriation of Jewish property in the burning of synagogues, in the murder of Jews on the

trumped up charge of ritual murder. Neither I nor
you have ever accused Jews of having been responsible for the death of Jesus. Yet we participate in these
horrendous crimes in proportion to which we do not
abjure them. And since so much of what occurred
was either promulgated by Church officials or at
least tolerated by them, it is necessary that the official Church speak out against those acts. Please,
Pope John Paul II, say that we are sorry, say that we
want to be cleansed of all of our guilt including that
for how we have historically, and in some cases currently, treated Jewish men and women, boys and
girls.

I will allude to certain specifics here, not because
I think that you are unaware of them but because,
based on my experience, "defenders" of the Church
(who, in failing to recognize our failures, are actually
"offenders") will say that I am merely generalizing,
even fantasizing. I—and Jewish people everywhere—wish this were only make believe. In 306
our church decreed that Christians and Jews could
not eat together. In 538, during Passion Week, Jews
were forbidden to be seen in the streets; in the next
century Christians were ordered not to consult with
Jewish doctors; later (1050), not to live in houses
which were owned by Jews. In 1179 Jews were not
allowed to witness against Christians in court. Jews
had to wear distinguishing identification on their
clothing (1215), were made to live in ghettos (1267),
could not earn academic degrees (1434); the list is
terribly long.

Church councils and synods forbade the construc-
tion of synagogues (1222), delegated Jews to pay
taxes equal to Christians for support of the Church
(1078), insisted that Christians could not sell or rent
real estate to Jews (1279)—again, the list is terribly,
terribly long. Raul Hilberg has succinctly summa-

rized the West's policy toward Jews, much of it origi-
nating with the Church, in his history, *The Destruction of the European Jews.* "Since the fourth century
after Christ, there have been three anti-Jewish policies: conversion, expulsion, annihilation. The second appeared as an alternative to the first, and the
third emerged as an alternative to the second." My
own fear is that a fourth disastrous policy will oc-
cur—indifference to the Jews. I am convinced that
you do not wish to have that happen, either. But
there is that ambiguity which troubles me.

Respectfully, but emphatically, I want to say that
visits to the United Nations, even to Israel, by popes
are seen as near empty gestures, public relations
events, unless they are backed by more substantial
works. After the Holocaust, in which much of Christian Europe participated in the annihilation of millions of Jews, visits with Waldheim are not con-
sistent with acts of peace and reconciliation with
Jews. Nor are certain passages in the Passion Play at
Oberammergau, nor is the silence surrounding
crimes perpetrated on the Jews by our coreligionists.

One suggestion that I have for an important symbolic gesture is the excommunication by the Church
of Adolph Hitler. I am aware that this would be a
first, a decree which would seem to be saying that a
dead man is cut off from the sacraments—a near
absurdity. But just as the Catholic Church has cor-
rected an injustice by rehabilitating Galileo in our
time, so too it would be appropriate to correct the
serious omission of having allowed Hitler to have
died on the tax roles of the Church. If a Catholic had
fought a duel in Nazi Germany, propositioned a
priest in the confessional, or divorced and remarried,
such a person would have been excommunicated.
Adolf Hitler was not. Such a decree from you now
would be a sign to Jews today about the seriousness

of the Church's attitude toward Jews; it would also
be a sign to the Ku Klux Klan, to neo-Nazis, to
hatemongers everywhere that the official Church
will not tolerate anti-Jewish behavior.

Jews and Christians alike are aware of the charge
of silence which hangs over the head of Pope Pius
XII whose own image hangs as an albatross about
the papacy's neck when the issue of Catholic-Jewish
relations is raised. Here again I feel that the acknowledgment of Vatican withdrawal from standing
firm on the subject of persecution of Jews must be
admitted and repented. The story of an encyclical
leaps to mind. Some of us are aware that in 1938
Pope Pius XI commissioned an encyclical letter to
be written for him by the U.S. Jesuit, John LaFarge.
Father LaFarge produced that document but before it
was published the Pope died. Cardinal Jean
Tisserant of the Roman Curia suggested that Pius XI
was murdered, poisoned by his doctor whose
daughter was Mussolini's mistress. When Eugenio
Pacelli assumed the chair of Peter as Pope Pius XII,
he issued an encyclical letter under the same title
with all of the references to antisemitism deleted.

It has been asked, would such an encyclical have
done any good? That is, of course, the wrong question. The moral center of Catholicism must speak
out on all major issues, at all times. Creating and
continuing a moral climate always "does good," for
now and for the future. But beyond that, we know
that when the Nazis implemented a euthanasia program, murdering the retarded, the handicapped, the
aged, Christian leaders spoke out in Germany and
the Nazis officially discontinued the effort. We can
only imagine how many lives would have been saved had your predecessor spoken firmly about Jewish
persecutions. Yes, we know that Dutch Catholics
were made to suffer by the Nazis when they aided

Jews. But the protest from the Church should have come long before that time. We need that encyclical now, late but better than not to have a pope's words at all.

Other actions are necessary as well. Seminaries need to be instructed to establish more courses in Catholic-Jewish relations, including the tragic aspects of that topic. New terms must be found for what are now referred to as the Old Testament and the New Testament. You yourself have suggested that Hebrew Scriptures and Christian Scriptures are appropriate alternatives. Please insist on such changes so that all of the supercessionist implications of the titles now in common use may be swept away. I would like to see our liturgical calendar revised to include an annual memorial service for the victims of the Holocaust. This will force preachers from the pulpit to deal with the issue.

Since World War II, I have never heard a single word uttered in a Catholic homily on the *Shoah*. I have heard sermons on the value of the Easter bunny, on why it is a sin for men to wear Bermuda shorts—but never on the murder of the 6,000,000; including 1,000,000 Jewish children not yet in their teens. We must, further, hear insistence on the Jewishness of Jesus, Mary, Joseph, the apostles, all of whom would have perished under the Nazis if the time of their existence had been different. I hope that you will emphasize the error of the attempts to missionize the Jews. You could recommend that traditional Catholic teaching on the meaning of history be re-examined. We are told that history is the revelation of God's plan for humanity and we cannot be blamed for asking: How does Auschwitz fit into such a plan?

I wish to go beyond this and request that you speak to certain words that have caused great injury, words

by men crowned as holy saints of our Church, yet
who shouted such unholy blasphemies against Jews.
I will quote just a few but as one reads these, one
must keep in mind that they are the words, not of a
Hitler or an Adolf Eichmann, not of a Rudolph Hoess
or a Joseph Goebbels, but of St. John Chrysostom, St.
Cyprian, St. Hippolytus, St. Ephraim, St. Gregory of
Nyssa—an abominably long list. Chrysostom first.
He called Jews "lustful, rapacious, greedy, perfidious
bandits"; saw them as "inveterate murderers, de-
stroyers, men possessed by the devil;" declaring that
"they have surpassed the ferocity of wild beasts, for
they murder their offspring and immolate them to
the devil." Cyprian before him insisted that the Jews
put Jesus to death and "Now the peoplehood of the
Jews has been cancelled." Hippolytus condemned
Jews "because they killed the son of their Benefac-
tor." Ephraim labeled the synagogue a "harlot" while
Gregory of Nyssa told of Jews as "Slayers of the lord,
murderers of the prophets, enemies of God, haters of
God, adversaries of grace, enemies of their father's
faith, advocates of the devil, brood of vipers, slan-
derers, scoffers, men of darkened minds, leaven of
Pharisees, congregation of demons, sinners, wicked
men, stoners, and haters of goodness." I cannot go on.
What we need is someone of your authority to dis-
avow these words and the myriad which are like
them, words which were spoken by churchmen and
which are found repeated today in publications of
hate groups as justification for their own sins. We
need you to tell us that certain Catholic teachers
have been wrong about the Jews. We need you to give
us an extraordinary message because, as the great
Catholic novelist, Flannery O'Connor, has said, "to
the hard of hearing you shout, and for the almost-
blind you draw large and startling figures." We need
you to say that antisemitism is damned by God, that

antisemitism is a God-damned thing. Make no ambiguous statement, leave no room for interpretation.

Frankly, your reception of Kurt Waldheim was, at
best, an ambiguous statement. It left room for interpretation. A second meeting with the Austrian
president would probably go from ambiguous to in-
flammatory. After that initial engagement, New
York's Cardinal O'Connor initiated a joint prayer
meeting between Christians and Jews to ease tension, as he said, "not to dialogue, not to give speeches
or argue or debate, but simply to pray together for
increased mutual understanding and peaceful resolution of a regrettable difference." Rabbi Marc Tanen-
baum favored the idea but added that such a service
"could not be a substitute for dealing with the funda-
mental issues that have been raised by the morally
incredible visit." Another high Church man, Cardinal Decourtray of Lyons, France, it was reported,
made it a point to visit his city's Holocaust museum
the day before you met with Waldheim. He also went
to the synagogue there. As the Catholic magazine
Commonweal editorialized, "It was a telling gesture,
and one that deserves to be emulated." When the
Grand Rabbi of Lyons expressed his anguish over the
Waldheim issue, Cardinal Decourtray is said to have
replied immediately: "This event is painful to me as
well. I ask myself what might have been the motives
leading to the decision. In all frankness, I do not
know."

We are told that Austrian Catholic bishops joined
Mr. Waldheim in pressuring the Vatican for the
meeting. This is particularly sad in the light of Austrian history, a history which must not be overlooked. In 1938, 185,000 Jews lived in that country.
When World War II ended, only 3,000 had survived.
That nation was often referred to as *Eretz hadomin*,
the land of blood, in Jewish chronicles of the Middle

Ages. In the very month that you met with Waldheim, the mayor of the city of Linz, in Austria, sent
an open letter to the World Jewish Congress in
which he supported his president against the charges
about his Nazi past. Wrote Linz: "... you must consider your claim the same as that of your brothers in
faith two thousand years ago, who had Jesus Christ
sent to death in a mock trial because he didn't fit
into the scheme of the masters of Jerusalem . . . As
it was left to a Roman to proclaim this unjust verdict then, this time you managed to find as the vic-
timizer the person in the American Justice Department who put Dr. Waldheim on the 'watch list.'" I
know of no Austrian Church official having de-
nounced Mayor Linz's words. We do know of many
Austrian voters who publicly boasted of voting for
Waldheim precisely because he may have had the
past of which he is now suspected. A syndicated
columnist in my country, Richard Cohn, wrote this
paragraph:

> Little wonder Austrians elected Waldheim their presi-
> dent. Their presidency is a symbolic office and Wal-
> dheim is a fitting symbol. Most Austrians supported
> unification with Nazi Germany, 550,000 out of
> 7,000,000 were Nazi Party members and Austrians
> played a major role in the killing of Jews. Austrians
> commanded four of the six main death camps and
> comprised one/third of the SS extermination units.

Then Mr. Cohn concludes: "There is no institution more dedicated to memory than the Catholic
Church. But in agreeing to see Waldheim, the pope
lent his moral authority to Waldheim's amoral
amnesia."

The late Jean Amery, a Holocaust survivor, wrote
in his book *1945: In Search of Europe* that he could
hardly comprehend the extent of Austria's historical
amnesia. And Gordon Craig has reminded us of how,

for over two decades after the Holocaust, "The period 1938–1945 was studiously avoided by Austrian historians, research on it being left for the most part to their foreign colleagues," and that this situation, which, Professor Botz has written, makes it "easier for Austria to repress any responsibility for its own Nazis," has not greatly improved since then. It is perhaps worth adding that the fact that the Christian OVP began as early as 1945 to work for a restoration of voting rights to Austrian Nazis—despite their disproportionately prominent role in Hitler's murder apparatus—shows a real facility for forgetting.

I am not here attempting to tar all Austrians with one brush. But I am emphasizing the importance of Waldheim the man, of Waldheim the symbol. When your meeting with him is put in context, it is at least embarrassing, more abhorrent in the greater regard. And, I repeat, a second meeting is incomprehensible. I must agree with the group of Protestant leaders led by the Rev. Dr. Franklin Littell who protested your initial encounter with Waldheim. "The invitation," they insisted, "disgraces the memory of Christian martyrs who opposed Nazi idolatry. The invitation dishonors the memory of the victims of the Nazi Holocaust." The ministers, representing six Christian denominations, conclude that "The wounds of the Lord's people cannot be so lightly healed." They are right to emphasize the wounds. How is it that the representative of Jesus the great healer can risk causing so much pain to a people already overwhelmed by pain? Surely this is not deliberate on your part. And yet Peter Hebblethwaite, writing in the National Catholic Reporter, can call the Waldheim affair "a spectacular departure from the traditions of 'prudence' that habitually governed Vatican diplomacy." He adds another important sentence:

"Not only is Jewish memory tenacious, but the distinction made by the Vatican between the spiritual relationship with Jews (we are of common stock) and the political relationship (we do not recognize the state of Israel) is unintelligible to most Jews."

Let me pick up this point, on the diplomatic recognition of the state of Israel. Permit me to point to your own words in your Apostolic Letter of April 20, 1984, *Redemptionis Anno:* "For the Jewish people," you stated, "who live in the State of Israel and who preserve in that land such precious testimonies of their history and their faith, we must ask for the desired security and the due tranquility that is the prerogative of every nation and condition of life and of progress for every society." And what of the statement from the Vatican Commission for Religious Relations with the Jews (May, 1985) which reads this way: "The existence of the State of Israel and its political options should be envisaged not in a perspective which is in itself religious, but in their reference to the common principles of international law." How can these words not be followed by other words, words which concretize the Vatican's diplomatic relations with Israel just as they are regularized with so many other countries? Recognition of Israel would be a healing gesture, a necessary gesture. It is not an ultimate kind of move, it would not—and should not—be perceived as an anti-Arab measure, it would be nothing extraordinary. What is extraordinary is the withholding of such recognition. This is in no way an anti-Arab position. I am not anti-Arab. I have written about equal rights for Arabs, about the glories of modern Arabic literature and been a member of AAUG, Arab American University Graduates. Recognition of Israel would not be anti-Arab. Surely we are not to be bound by the words of Msgr. Domenico Tardini, a top Vatican aide, who during the war said this: "And the question of Holy Places? Palestine is by this time more sacred for Catholics than . . . for Jews." To be silent on the subject of the legitimacy of Israel now is to reflect on an earlier silence, one which helped doom Jews during the Nazi period.

A correspondent reported that, late in the war, Pope Pius XII was asked why he had not spoken out on the persecution of the Jews, and that the pontiff replied this way: "Dear friend, do not forget that millions of Catholics serve in the German armies. Shall I bring them into conflicts of conscience?" The fact is that the Vatican did break silence a number of times. It reacted against the Russian invasion of Finland and Pius expressed concern over the German invasions of Holland, of Belgium, of Luxembourg. He even asked President Roosevelt for protection from possible Allied bombing of Rome. But for the Jews? Silence. There was a significant number of Catholics who helped to save Jewish lives during this period, but nearly all acted independently, without direction of spiritual leaders. Where churchmen helped Jews they far too often only cared about baptized Jews. These are the unhappy facts of our recent history, facts which we must acknowledge, facts which we must repent.

Is it any wonder then that the great Greek writer Nikos Kazantzakis sadly observed that everywhere you touch a Jew you find a wound. There is another dimension to this as well. Everywhere you touch a calendar, you find a date in history when the Jewish people have suffered profound wounds. This is remarkably illustrated in Simon Wiesenthal's moving book titled *Every Day Remembrance Day*. The volume is a mournful chronicle of Jewish martyrdom through history. For every day of the year there are listed here many events in Jewish history for which

a kaddish might be said: every day; many entries. So
many of these atrocities were committed by church-
goers that the cumulative effect is stunning, terrifying to us as Christians. Let me choose Wiesenthal's
entries for just one date, May 18, your birthdate, as
an example.

- 1096 Troops of the First Crusade arrive in Worms
  on the Rhine, Germany. The wealthy Jews receive
  protection—after payment—from the bishop of
  Worms in his own castle. The other 500 Jews, who
  stay in their houses, are slaughtered. The town is
  looted and the Torah scrolls are burned. Among
  the victims are Rabbi Solomon and his family.
- 1721 An auto-da-fe is held in Madrid, Spain, where
  descendants of forcibly baptized Jews are accused
  of being "Judaizers," secretly practicing the Jewish
  religion. Among the victims is an old woman of
  94, Maria Barbara Carillo, who is burned alive.
- 1919 During a three-day pogrom, 14 Jews are massacred, 9 wounded, and 15 Jewish women and girls
  are raped in Ivankov in the district of Kiev,
  Ukraine, by units under the command of Struk, ally
  of Simon Petlyura and the Ukrainian National
  Army.
- 1942 During a large-scale Aktion, 180 Jews are
  shot and 350 are deported to labor camps from the
  ghetto of Tlumacz, Ukrainian S.S.R. The Germans
  arrest 2,000 Jews from the Wolkovysk ghetto in
  the Polish province of Grodno (today Belorussian
  S.S.R.), and kill them outside of town. This gives
  rise to a Jewish underground, which works with
  the partisans in the forest. Deported to the Sobibor
  extermination camp are 1,000 Jews from the Sied-
  liszcze ghetto in Poland.
- 1943 Jewish internees numbering 2,511 are sent
  from the Westerbork transit camp in the Dutch
  province of Drenthe to Sobibor.

• 1944 From Vienna, 4 Jews are deported to the
Theresienstadt concentration camp in Czechoslovakia. Having deported 160 Jews from the Drancy
transit camp in France, the Nazis shoot them in
the Provanovska labor camp in Kaunas, Lithua-
nian S.S.R.

Every date is unfortunately filled with such information in this book, and we know that even so,
every Jewish tragedy has not been recorded by historians—though recorded by God we are certain.
These events weigh heavily on every Jewish soul.
We must not be unmindful of the words of Elie
Wiesel which he has chiseled on our consciousness
in referring to the Holocaust: While not every victim was a Jew, every Jew was a victim. We need to
make a Christian response to these sad, sad occur-
rences.

Let me remind you of your own words spoken in
Manchester, England in 1982: ". . . I wish to reiterate the full respect of the Catholic Church for the
Jewish people throughout the world. In the Spirit of
the Second Vatican Council, I recall the desire of the
Church to collaborate willingly with you in the
great cause of mankind, knowing that we have a
common tradition that honours the sanctity of God
and calls us to love the Lord our God with all our
heart and with all our soul." And to the executive
committee of the National Council of Christians
and Jews you spoke against discrimination: "To single out and denounce such facts and stand together
against them is a noble act and a proof of our mutual
brotherly commitment," you said. Furthermore,
your visit to the synagogue in Rome was an important message in itself and your speech there was a
healing one, repudiating any notion that Jews were
guilty of killing Jesus. I do not want to minimize
efforts such as that. But the beauty and value of such

deeds are minimized by an act such as a meeting with Mr. Waldheim.

What we need now is a pope who is more than just an ordinary occupant of the chair of Peter. We need a hero. I have said many times that the term "heroic Christianity" is redundant. All Christians are called to be heroes. Do not blame us if we ask for a leadership that might help make better Christians of all of the people of our faith, if we ask for a leadership that might lead us all to be heroic men and women in our faith. Any concept of heroism, however, rejects any notion of ambiguity. Give us unambiguous gestures of which it will be unnecessary to ask, "What did the pope mean by that?" Give us acts and words to which we can easily respond with "Yes" and "I see." The Catholic Church's relations with the Jewish people may well be the measure by which the Catholic Church will be judged. If true, some of us tremble in fear of that judgment. Because we love the Church, we ask for leadership. Because we love the Church, we ask for repentance. Because we love the Church, we ask for this immediate sign: Abort your scheduled second meeting with Waldheim. It would be a holy abortion. Then, please follow this with more signs.

Peace in deed,

Harry James Cargas

On Interviewing

Holocaust Survivors

Before the St. Louis Oral History Society was founded, I had interviewed many Holocaust survivors. When the society invited me to cooperate with them I was able to share some of what I had learned and to gain a great deal on how to improve my own technique, especially guided by the wisdom of Dr. Moisy Shopper, a skilled psychoanalyst. Here is a compilation of what I have discovered about conducting oral history discussions from my own experiences and those of others. It was published in *Martyrdom and Resistance* and is presented in honor of Molly Clark Cargas, our beloved daughter-in-law.

As survivors of the Holocaust now grow collectively older, many seem to be aware that if they do not tell their stories, the full truth of what happened at Auschwitz, at Buchenwald, at Dachau and at Treblinka may be in danger of being lost. Therefore many of these women and men are more willing to share their World War II experiences for the record. As a result of this development, increasingly more individuals and groups are committed to taping interviews with survivors to bring a more complete history of the Holocaust into focus. It is my experience, as an interviewer of survivors, at first acting alone, and later as a member of the St. Louis Oral History

Project (under the auspices of the St. Louis Center for Holocaust Studies), that too many interviewers may rush into a taping session before being adequately prepared to do so. Thus, the meetings become less useful than they might, even become counterproductive on occasion because a survivor might get "turned off" by the incident and refuse to be very cooperative on the first or even subsequent interviews. The seriousness of such an encounter cannot be overstressed, and neither can the preparation for it. I would like to make certain suggestions and observations for potential interviewers to consider, based on my work and the work of others I know, in this important effort.

There are basically three time periods to look at: preparatory to an interview, the meeting itself, the follow-up. Each is important and not to be slighted.

Preparing *for* *the* *Interview*

Before an interview, there is need of much preparation. Foremost is the need to know your subject. Study, in quite some detail, the history of World War II and the actual events of the Holocaust itself. (If you need a starting point, you can begin with Raul Hilberg's *The Destruction of the European Jews* or Nora Levin's *The Holocaust.* For additional suggestions you could consult my work published by The American Library Association, *The Holocaust: An Annotated Bibliograpy* with 425 titles described.) To enter into a dialogue with a survivor while being basically ignorant of the events of the era about which you hope to be talking will inevitably prove disastrous.

Organizing, Phrasing Questions

Organize a series of questions that you plan to ask. These should be of two types: general and specific. Among the former might be such questions as "What has it meant to you to be a survivor?" "Are you angry today?" "Are you hopeful for the future?" "What has America meant to you?" "What does the State of Israel mean to you?" (This last is intended, of course, specifically for Jewish survivors, as will be a number of questions.) Of the more specific kind are: "When were you imprisoned?" "What was your family life like?" "How did you survive?" (This question must be asked in a particularly non-threatening way since survivors are sometimes asked this question in a tone which implies that the only way one could have continued to live was by cooperating somehow with the enemy. Perhaps a better way to phrase it would be "What were the circumstances that made it possible for you to live?") Another important discussion prompter is this: "How has your experience influenced your religion?"

Try to obtain some good maps of Europe and of the areas, if you can ascertain them beforehand, in which your interviewee was raised, was imprisoned in a ghetto, was incarcerated in a camp, etc. A map illustrating placements of the various prison and death camps would also prove helpful.

Initial contact is probably best made with the prospective interviewee by letter. Explain what you want to talk about and what your qualifications are, which group you are associated with, etc. Give the person you are contacting the opportunity to refuse your invitation. There are some survivors who simply are unwilling, for a variety of legitimate reasons, to discuss the Holocaust, particularly with strangers. Allow for this with care so that you don't make them feel guilty for having turned you down. One of

your goals is to help unburden these men and wom-
en, not to add to their enormous emotional load.

Follow the letter with a telephone call some three
to four days later. If your person agrees to meet with
you, arrange for a time and place. The location of the
interview is important. It must be in surroundings
in which both of you are comfortable. Almost always, in my encounters, I find that you will be invited to your interviewee's home. In general, that
seems to be by far the very best site. Choose a time
which will allow you a prolonged, no rush, uninter-
rupted visit—a time free from the bustle of scurry-
ing teenagers, telephone rings and the like. Sunday
morning is often a good choice.

Finally, as far as the preliminaries are concerned,
be fully prepared. Know your subject, as previously
indicated. If possible, take two tape recorders which
are in tested working order and be sure to have more
than enough cassettes with you. It is discouraging to
be in the middle of a very sensitive dialogue and
have to interrupt it because you failed to have the
adequate amount of tapes. You can almost never
"pick up again where we left off" on a subsequent
visit. One other point of preparation: be prepared to
be shocked, to be bored (by a repetition of stories, by
autobiographical details which may have no bearing
on what you are trying to do—although you can be
fooled on what turns out, finally, to have value), to
be fully trusted (with all of the baggage that goes
with it), to be only partially trusted (by a skeptical
survivor who may want to know why you are really
doing this—what's in it for you?) Your task is to
listen. Prepare yourself to listen well.

Now we come to the actual interview. It is important that you go alone for your appointment. Another person, even a friend of the person you are
visiting with, can prove quite distracting. You are

attempting to build up a relationship with your person, and another individual simply breaks the mood too often. You are asking the survivor to trust you and that is difficult enough. To ask that such trust be extended to another may be unrealistic. The only time a third person might be in on an interview is if that person is a spouse of the interviewee. Very often the spouse too will be a survivor and some of the best sessions I've heard are with a wife and husband. The interaction between the two of them may at times prove extremely informative.

You can begin the discussion by showing the maps which you brought, asking the survivor to indicate places of autobiographical importance to her or him. Let them teach you. Do not go in like the big Holocaust expert, even if your knowledge of the field is wide. You don't know what this individual went through and you wish to find out. If you are perceived as a know-it-all or as one who is interviewing only to validate certain preconceived theories, your encounter is doomed.

Play Back the Tape

After a few minutes around the maps, however you begin, it might be a good idea to play the tape back to your interviewee. There is something comforting, less threatening to the person when the voice can be monitored. Somehow a little of the mystery of technology disappears and any elimination of barriers is to be welcomed.

Several important "don'ts" must be stressed. First, don't be in a hurry. Show that you are relaxed. Help create a calm atmosphere. This will allow for a much better climate of response to you and therefore to your questions. Second, unless specifically asked, do not "help" a person who is groping for words, struggling for language. Just take it easy. The word being searched for eventually comes. If you don't come off as a language expert or a superior (therefore threatening) intellect, you won't run the risk of a wrong, even insulting guess, or of planting your ideas into the minds of the speakers. Third, don't interrupt the flow of words to ask for clarification, to get the spelling of a word, to ask for a repeat of a word you don't understand. Make a note and come back to your new questions later. Finally, don't stick rigorously to the order of questions you have prepared. Answers to some of your questions will, if you are alert, lead to new queries which you will wish to put to them. Do so and later come back to those still to be covered from the list you brought with you.

Do Not Rush Interview

Now a few "do's." Do allow for pauses and for silences. Oftentimes a person will have a better answer to your inquiry than the first one given. Or a reformulation, an elaboration, will bring out wonderfully new and thoughtful information. Staccato interviews, quick question followed by quick reply in rat-at-at-at fashion, are the worst kind. Media interviewers are terrified of pauses, of "dead air" on their programs. That's why most of them are so vacuous. But you don't have to be in a rush; important answers usually take time. Another do: do pay attention to what your interviewee is saying. Many of your best questions in the session will be based on something which your new friend has just said. Follow the lead and go with it. You can always return later to your prepared questions. Also, in paying attention, you may find that you will better be able to get at what is meant as well as what is said. For example, sometimes someone will say something like, "I don't want to talk about it" in a way which is actually testing you. What may be meant is "I do want to talk about it if you think you can take this dreadful account." Be alert for this kind of statement. If a person says, "It isn't important but . . ." this may well be a signal that it is indeed important to the narrator. Follow it through. Also keep an eye on the tape. Don't let the best part of the interview be lost because the cassette was used up three minutes earlier! Do be certain to get the correct spelling of family names, place names, foreign expressions used during the interview. There will be time to do that towards the end, from your notes, as the encounter is winding down. Do ask to see any artifacts, documents or letters that your person might be willing to share with you, and ask for the stories behind each. Finally, do learn when not to turn off the tape recorder. Sometimes a few of the best insights will be given you as you are saying good-bye at the door. You may hear, "Oh, I forgot to mention . . ." or some such lead in. Get it on tape. It could be of great value in the interview.

And last there is the post-interview period, the follow-up. Immediately as you can, after your visit, try to recall if anything of importance was said before the tape recorder was started or after it was turned off. Note down on paper anything that might prove of value later. If you were shown artifacts, describe them, comment on the way they were presented, etc.

Transcribe	You should begin to transcribe the tape, verbatim, as
Tape	soon as is convenient. One reason is that you will
Quickly	still have the rhythm, the pronunciation of the sur-

vivor's speech fresh in your mind. This may be necessary for understanding certain terms and expressions
which the recorder may have fuzzed. And, remember, the tape is actually the document you had
sought. It contains so much more than any transcrip-
tion because it has tone of voice, silences, sighs,
weeping—so much more is communicated via the
tape than via the typewriter to someone who wasn't
there.

Following   Members of the St. Louis Oral History Project have
Up   found that survivors welcome follow-up phone calls
the   from interviewers. After all, new friendships have
Interview   been made; a bond ought to be kept up. Very personal secrets, in many cases, were revealed during the
discussions and to drop the relationship immediately may result in feelings being seriously hurt. When
appropriate, a New Year card or a birthday greeting
(you'll probably have that anniversary on your tape)
is recommended.

One important caution remains. No individual
should interview survivors too often. I know one
man who had wide experience in doing interviews
with writers (which he published) and with the famous and not so well known on his television programs (covering a seven-year period). He interviewed
twelve survivors in two and a half months for a pro-
jected book and he was absolutely burned out. Some
of his tapes have yet to be transcribed (after over four
years) and the book is going nowhere. My suggestion
is each interviewer limit the number done to about
two or three per year, spaced at least several months
apart. The dialogues are very emotionally draining.
This is perhaps more apparent regarding the survivors, but observation proves this to be true of the
inquirers as well.

A Holocaust Commemoration

Liturgy is important for the soul. It is necessary. Therefore I offer this Christian commemoration which was initially published by the United States Holocaust Memorial Council, then in *Liturgy* magazine, and most recently in a compilation by Marcia Sachs Littell, *Liturgies on the Holocaust* (1986). Msgr. Joseph Bailey honors me by permitting me to dedicate this to him.

Narrator   We come together for this memorial service to remember. Re-member means to bring certain events of the past together again, to make them whole in order that they may not be forgotten. We must make efforts not to let the great tragedy of the Holocaust slip from the mind of the world or to slip from our minds individually. For if the Holocaust is forgotten, the way will be paved for another, perhaps a final destruction of all of humanity. The massacre of six million Jews must not be a prelude to a future disaster. Our attitude toward the Holocaust may well determine that of our children and of our children's children. What we do today (this evening), now, is of extreme importance.

We pay homage to the dead in what must be seen

as momentous Christian tragedy. If Dr. Martin
Luther King, Jr., was right when he insisted that
racism is really a white people's problem then we
are correct in witnessing to the Holocaust as a
Christian problem. It was in traditionally Christian
nations that the murders took place. Many Christians died at the death camps of Auschwitz, Dora,
Bergen-Belsen and the rest, and we gather today (this
evening) to re-member these non-Jewish dead as
well. Yet some non-Jews were able to save themselves by espousing the Nazi cause. No Jew was allowed to do so. While Poles and Germans and
French and others were victims of Hitler's policies,
only the Jews were victims of victims; that is, only
Jews were singled out for killing by Poles and Germans and French and others.

Think of it! How many people does it take to kill
six million Jews and perhaps an equal number of
non-Jews as well? Who even thought of the plan of
trying to rid the world of every Jewish woman, man,
and child? Who thought of ovens for human beings
while living in nations committed to Jesus Christ,
called the Prince of Peace? Who designed the ovens
and the gas chambers? Who engineered them, bribed
high government officials to gain the murderous
contracts? Who operated the demonic facilities, re-
paired them when they broke down, studied their
operations to make them more efficient? When Nazi
troops conquered countries, and did not know which
people were Jews and which were not, who pointed
out the Jews to the invaders?

The question remains. How many people does it
take to cooperate in such a large scale slaughter?

And who among us can be certain that if we were
in the wrong place at the wrong time, we too might
cooperate with the forces of evil? Are we, in some
way, doing exactly that by our subtle racism, our

lack of interest in war-torn nations around the world, our deliberate ignorance of genocide through starvation that some people are experiencing as we sit here, this very moment?

Let us beg the Lord God for forgiveness and make a firm purpose of amendment,

Thirty-second Meditation

Written in pencil in the sealed railway-car
  here in this carload
  i am eve
  with abel my son
  if you see my other son
  cain son of man
  tell him i

*First Reader
(a woman)*
                    —Dan Pagis (translated from the Hebrew
                                by Stephen Mitchell)

Narrator

The mother speaking in this poem did not have time to complete her thought. Death was too eager to take her. She went to her end like so many mothers and children without having a chance at life.

*Second Reader
(a child)*

These words were written by a young Jewish girl, imprisoned in a ghetto:

The Garden
  A little garden,
  Fragrant and full of roses.
  The path is narrow
  And a little boy walks along it.

  A little boy, a sweet boy,
  Like that growing blossom.
  When the blossom comes to bloom,
  The little boy will be no more.
                          —Franta Bass

Narrator   Over one million Jewish children under the age of twelve lost their lives in the Holocaust.

Third Reader (a man)   And so a long line is formed in the front of the orphanage on Sliska Street. A long procession, children, small, tiny, rather precocious, emaciated, weak, shriveled and shrunk. They carry shabby packages, some have school-books, note-books under their arms. No one is crying.

Slowly they go down the steps, line up in rows, in perfect order and discipline, as usual. Their little eyes are turned toward the doctor. They are strangely calm; they feel almost well. The doctor is going with them, so what do they have to be afraid of? They are not alone, they are not abandoned.

Dr. Janusz Korczak busies himself with the children with a sober earnestness. He buttons the coat of one child, ties up a package of another, or straightens the cap of a third. Then he wipes off a tear which is rolling down the thin little face of a child. . . .

Then the procession starts out. It is starting out for a trip from which—everybody feels it—one never comes back. All these young, budding lives. . . . And all this is marching quietly and orderly to the place of their untimely doom.

The children are calm, but inwardly they must feel it, they must sense it intuitively. Otherwise how could you explain the deadly seriousness on their pale little faces? But they are marching quietly in orderly rows, calm and earnest, and at the head of them is Janusz Korczak.

All in
Unison
(or Narrator
and
congregation
alternate
stanzas)

Psalm 79

God, the pagans have invaded your heritage,
they have desecrated your holy Temple;
they have left the corpses of your servants
to the birds of the air for food,
and the flesh of your devout to the beasts of the earth

They have shed blood like water
throughout Jerusalem, not a gravedigger left!
we are now insulted by our neighbors,
butt and laughing-stock of all those around us.
How much longer will you be angry, Yahweh? For
    ever?
Is your jealousy to go on smouldering like a fire?

Pour out your anger on the pagans,
    who do not acknowledge you,
and on those kingdoms
    that do not call on your name,
for they have devoured Jacob
    and reduced his home to desolation.
Do not hold our ancestors' crimes against us,
in tenderness quickly intervene,
we can hardly be crushed lower;
help us, God our savior,
for the honor of your name;
Yahweh, blot out our sins,
rescue us for the sake of your name.

Why should the pagans ask, "Where is their God?"
May we soon see the pagans learning what vengeance
you exact for your servants' blood shed here!
May the groans of the captive reach you;
by your mighty arm rescue those doomed to die!

Pay our neighbors sevenfold, strike to the heart
for the monstrous insult proferred to you, Lord!
And we your people, the flock that you pasture,
    giving you everlasting thanks,
    will recite your praises for ever and ever.

Fourth   *O the Chimneys*
Reader   O the chimneys
(a woman)   On the ingeniously devised habitations of death
                      When Israel's body drifted as smoke
                      Through the air—
                      Was welcomed by a star, a chimney sweep,
                      A star that turned black
                      Or was it a ray of sun?

                      Oh the Chimneys!
                      Freedomway for Jeremiah and Job's dust—
                      Who devised you and laid stone upon stone
                      The road for refugees of smoke?

                      O the habitations of death,
                      Invitingly appointed
                      For the host who used to be a guest—
                      O you fingers
                      Laying the threshold
                      Like a knife between life and death—

                      O you chimneys,
                      O you fingers
                      And Israel's body as smoke through the air!
                          —Nelly Sachs, from *In the Habitations of Death*

Fifth Reader   As it began to grow light, the fire was lit in two of the
(a man)   pits in which about 2,500 dead bodies lay piled one on
                  top of the other. Two hours later all that could be
                  discerned in the white-hot flames were countless
                  charred and scorched shapes, the blackish-phosphores-
                  cent hue a sign that they were in an advanced stage of
                  cremation. At this point the fire had to be kept going
                  from outside because the pyre which at first protruded
                  about half a metre above the edge of the pit had, in the
                  meantime, gone below this level. While in the cre-
                  matorium ovens, once the corpses were thoroughly
                  alight, it was possible to maintain a lasting red heat
                  with the help of fans, in the pits the fire would burn
                  only as long as the air could circulate freely in be-
                  tween the bodies. As the heap of bodies settled, no air

was able to get in from outside. This meant that we stokers had constantly to pour oil or wood alcohol on the burning corpses, in addition to human fat, large quantities of which had collected and was boiling in the two collecting pans on either side of the pit. The sizzling fat was scooped out with buckets on a long curved rod and poured all over the pit causing flames to leap up amid much crackling and hissing. Dense smoke and fumes rose incessantly. The air reeked of oil, fat, benzole and burnt flesh.

—Filip Muller, *Eyewitness Auschwitz*

Narrator   Master of the universe, help us to bear in mind always our potential for evil. And strengthen us, our God, so that we may fulfill our potential for good instead.

Sixth Reader (a man)   One day when we came back from work, we saw three gallows rearing up in the assembly place, three black crows. Roll call. SS all around us, machine guns trained: the traditional ceremony. Three victims in chains—and one of them, the little servant, the sad-eyed angel.

The SS seemed more preoccupied, more disturbed than usual. To hang a young body in front of thousands of spectators was no light matter. The head of the camp read the verdict. All eyes were on the child. He was lividly pale, almost calm, biting his lips. The gallows threw its shadow over him.

This time the Lagerkapo refused to act as executioner. Three SS replaced him.

The three necks were placed at the same moment within the nooses.

"Long live liberty!" cried the two adults.

But the child was silent.

"Where is God? Where is He?" someone behind me asked.

At a sign from the head of the camp, the three chairs tipped over.

Total silence through the camp. On the horizon, the sun was setting.

"Bare your heads!" yelled the head of the camp. His voice was raucous. We were weeping.

"Cover your heads!"

Then the march past began. The two adults were no longer alive. Their tongues hung swollen, blue-tinged. But the third rope was still moving; being so light, the child was still alive. . . .

For more than half an hour he stayed there, struggling between life and death, dying in slow agony under our eyes. And we had to look him full in the face. He was still alive when I passed in front of him. His tongue was still red, his eyes were not yet glazed.

Behind me, I heard the same man asking:

"Where is God now?"

And I heard a voice within me answer him:

"Where is He? Here He is—He is hanging here on this gallows. . . ."

That night the soup tasted of corpses.

—Elie Wiesel, *Night*

Seventh Reader (a woman) If as Christians we thought that Church and Synagogue no longer affected one another, everything would be lost. And where this separation between the community and the Jewish nation has been made complete, it is the Christian community which has suffered. The whole reality of the revelation of God is then secretly denied. . . .

For in the person of the Jew there stands a witness before our eyes, the witness of God's covenant with Abraham, Isaac and Jacob and in that way with us all. Even one who does not understand Holy Scripture can see this reminder.

And don't you see, the remarkable theological importance, the extraordinary spiritual and sacred significance of the National Socialism that now lies behind us is that right from its roots it was antisemitic, that in this movement it was realized with a simply demonic clarity, that *the* enemy is the *Jew*. Yes, the enemy in this matter had to be a Jew. In this Jewish nation there really lives to this day the extraordinariness of the revelation of God. . . .

When the Christian Church confesses Jesus Christ as Savior and the Servant of God for us, for all men, also for the mighty majority of those who have no direct connection with the People Israel, then it does not confess Him *although* He was a Jew. . . .

No, we must strictly consider that Jesus Christ, in whom we believe, whom we Christians out of the heathen call our Savior and praise as the consummator of God's work on our behalf—He was *of Necessity a Jew*. We cannot be blind to this fact; it belongs to the concrete reality of God's work and of his revelation.

The problem of Israel is, since the problem of Christ is inseparable from it, the problem of existence as such. The man who is ashamed of Israel is ashamed of Jesus Christ and therefore of his own existence.

The attack on Judah means the attack on the rock of the work and revelation of God, beside which work and which revelation there is no other.

—Karl Barth, *Dogmatics in Outline*

Homily   (A brief homily by a pastor is in order here. Perhaps two short talks would be appropriate, one by a Christian minister, one by a rabbi.)

Narrator   Holocaust survivor and author Elie Wiesel has said
this:

> If someone suffers and he keeps silent, it can be a
> good silence. If someone suffers and I keep silent, then
> it's a destructive silence. If we envisage literature and
> human destiny as endeavors by man to redeem him-
> self, then we must admit the obsession, the overall
> dominating theme of responsibility, that we are re-
> sponsible for one another. I am responsible for his or
> her suffering, for his or her destiny. If not, we are
> condemned by our solitude forever and it has no
> meaning. This solitude is a negative, destructive soli-
> tude, a self-destructive solitude.
>   —From *Harry James Cargas in Conversation*
>   *with Elie Wiesel*

Eighth   Indeed we may not remain silent in view of the hor-
Reader   ror of the Holocaust. And yet we must choose our
words carefully. We must not oversentimentalize
the tragedy, we must not treat it with irreverence.
How, then, are we to speak out? Rabbi Irving Green-
berg has given us this guide: "Let us offer, then, as a
working principle the following. No statement, theological or otherwise, should be made that would
not be credible in the presence of burning children."

Narrator   There are times also, for silence, silence in the face
of the awesome proportions of the tragedy of the
Holocaust. We arrive at such a time now, as we ask
six Holocaust survivors from our community [or, if
this is not possible, six diverse members of the com-
munity] to each light a candle, one candle to repre-
sent one million Jewish dead, the totality, when lit,
to symbolize all those who died in the Holocaust.
    When the candles are lit, the overhead lights will

be extinguished for two minutes while we each offer our own prayers. When the electric lights are turned back on, you may, of course, continue to pray, but when you do begin to leave, please do so quietly.

Lighting of the Candles

Lowering of the Lights (two minutes)

Lights Back On

Dismissal

HARRY JAMES CARGAS is professor of literature and language at Webster University in St. Louis, Missouri. He is associate and founding editor of *Holocaust and Genocide Studies* and has published extensively on Christianity and the Holocaust. His books include *Harry James Cargas in Conversation with Elie Wiesel*, *A Christian Response to the Holocaust*, *Encountering Myself: Contemporary Christian Meditations*, *When God and Man Failed: Non-Jewish Views of the Holocaust*, and *The Holocaust: An Annotated Bibliography*.

The manuscript was prepared for publication by Christina Postema. The book was designed by Jim Billingsley. The typeface for the text and the display is Trump Mediaeval. The book is printed on 55-lb. Glatfelter text paper and is bound in Holliston Mills Roxite Linen. Manufactured in the United States of America.